D1273684

KINGS

&

CAPTAINS

KINGS
&
CAPTAINS

Variations on a Heroic Theme

Charles Moorman

The University Press of Kentucky

Standard Book Number 8131-1248-6
Library of Congress Catalog Card Number 78-147858

Copyright © 1971 by the University Press of Kentucky

A statewide cooperative scholarly publishing agency serving Berea
College, Centre College of Kentucky, Eastern Kentucky University,
Kentucky State College, Morehead State University, Murray State
University, University of Kentucky, University of Louisville, and
Western Kentucky University.

Editorial and Sales Offices: Lexington, Kentucky 40506

F M

For Ruth

Contents

PREFACE   *ix*

ACKNOWLEDGMENTS   *xiii*

Chapter One
THE ILIAD   *1*

Chapter Two
THE ODYSSEY   *30*

Chapter Three
BEOWULF   *57*

Chapter Four
THE SONG OF ROLAND   *87*

Chapter Five
THE NIBELUNGENLIED   *109*

Chapter Six
THE ICELANDIC SAGAS   *132*

Chapter Seven
THE ARTHUR LEGEND   *148*

NOTES   *173*

INDEX   *185*

Preface

In reading the scholarship and criticism devoted to what is generally called the heroic literature of the western world, one is frequently more puzzled by the problems that are ignored than by those that are dwelt upon. One can find in the works of generations of scholars pages devoted to explaining away every inconsistency in Homer, relating Beowulf to the hero of the Bear's Son's Tale, or debating the merits of the free-prose and book-prose theories of the origin of the Icelandic sagas—all of which are admittedly of great value to the study of the works—but he looks in vain for answers to questions that often puzzle the untutored upon a first reading. Why, for example, if Beowulf really believes in the *comitatus* code, does he desert Hygelac in battle? Or if Roland does not consider it heroic to summon aid at the beginning of the battle of Roncevaux, why does he later consider it proper to do so? Or what is in the least heroic in Achilles' sulking in his tent while his Greek companions are being slaughtered on the battlefield?

However naive such questions may seem to those concerned with the more technical problems of source and transmission and structure, they can and should lead to an occasional reexamination and revaluation of the great works of the western heroic tradition, those classics to which we have become so accustomed and about which there exists such critical unanimity that we have become content to rest happily in the inherited judgments of the masters.

Not that there has not been and does not continue to be critical dissension concerning the *Iliad* and the *Song of Ro-*

land and *Beowulf.* The "Homeric question," the origins of the *chansons de geste,* and the relative importance of Christianity and paganism in *Beowulf* are still active topics for debate and engender lifelong enmities among the learned. But in the detailed arguments among the Unitarians, Separatists, and Analysts, in the discussions of the chronology of Bronze Age history, even in the patently literary studies of the *Odyssey* by Howard W. Clarke and the *Iliad* by C. M. Bowra, many basic questions remain largely ignored. After all, just what *is* so heroic about Achilles' conduct, or Agamemnon's for that matter, in the wretched squabble over a slave girl that opens the *Iliad?* " 'You drunken sot,' [Achilles] cried, 'with the eyes of a dog and the courage of a doe! You never have the pluck to arm yourself and go into battle with the men or join the other captains in an ambush—you would sooner die!' " And who does not, despite the critics, honestly agree and sympathize with the sensible Oliver rather than the apparently monomaniacal Roland? And is not Beowulf in deserting his beloved lord and uncle, the "my Hygelac" whom he constantly praises, in Hygelac's death struggle a coward and a traitor by the standards of the *Battle of Maldon?*

A fresh look at these heroic works can be both purgative and instructional, especially if we abandon the conventions and restrictions of genre criticism and literary history and so avoid what Bowra calls the "obstructing prepossessions and distorting loyalties of professional scholars." Not that the discoveries and opinions of scholars and critics are not relevant and useful; one would be lost without them. But a reexamination *in vacuo* of these masterworks may reveal patterns and themes obscured by the scholarly convention that makes them conform to a preformed definition of a genre or to a preconceived tradition of literary development.

This study, then, attempts no more than its subtitle suggests; it advances the theory that the similar circumstances surrounding the composition of these works resulted in a characteristic point of view toward the heroic attitude and its place in society which, though slightly modified by particular conditions from age to age, in turn produced a series of variations upon a common theme—the opposition of king and captain, of responsible administrator and freebooting hero. The study makes no pretentions either to redefining the heroic genre or to rewriting literary history, however tempting occasionally the inclination to do so. Nor does it attempt to solve in any definitive way the complex technical problems of epic origin and transmission over which so much scholarly ink has been spilt, though it does occasionally utilize them.

If I may be permitted a personal word, I should like to state that I tend to think of myself as an essayist rather than as a scholar or critic. My method of approaching these works is thus eclectic, even contradictory at times, making use as it does of whatever tools—literary history, social and political history, myth, genre, etc.—seem appropriate at the moment. Like the traditionally objective scholar, I have occasionally weighed opposing scholarly theories; yet unlike the scholar, I have felt free to choose among the alternatives or even to offer compromise solutions on the admittedly subjective grounds of literary expediency. Like the New Critics, I am essentially examining each work as though it were autonomous, as though it contained entirely within itself the reason that it is so and not otherwise; yet unlike the New Critics, I have brought to bear upon the work whatever outside information I felt to be illuminating or helpful to interpretation.

This strategy, maddening as it must be to the academic purist, seems to me perfectly proper for the essayist, who is after all only a seeker, an experimenter, not a scientist or an advocate. And it is also the proper strategy, I think, for a volume which is intended not only for the specialist (if he will forego his professional irritation), but also for the non-specialist, the general student of literature who finds himself drawn back again and again to those masterpieces which have fostered and shaped the western heroic tradition and which have borne offspring—some robust and hearty, some crippled and perverted—in every age.

Acknowledgments

A portion of the *Beowulf* chapter of this study was originally published in *Modern Language Quarterly,* and I am grateful to the editors of that journal for their permission to reprint.

While it is impossible for me to acknowledge here all the advice and help I received in the preparation of this study, I should like to thank President W. D. McCain of the University of Southern Mississippi for his continued and generous support of my research and my beloved wife whose devotion and support no formal dedication can adequately repay.

KINGS

&

CAPTAINS

CHAPTER ONE

The Iliad

It is revealing to listen to the comments of undergraduates who come to the *Iliad* without awe and without prior knowledge of its content and tradition except perhaps for a vague notion that it is in some way heroic. For their first impression is not at all what one would expect, the usual mixture of respect and boredom with which students begin an assigned "classic," but instead a shocked amusement followed by a mounting interest in the narrative. Perversely enough, too, such students are not in the least put off by the details of battle, for which most critics seem compelled to apologize; furthermore, they are not in the least disturbed by the interference of the gods or by the constantly repeated epithets or by all the other devices which scholars regard as the dated, though historically justifiable, devices of an ancient poet. They will even swallow whole the catalog of ships in Book 2, regarding it, like any other piece of exposition, as a necessary part of the story, happily unaware that it was probably once a separate work and so might be regarded as detachable from the main.

It is not at all necessary, or even very profitable, to approach the *Iliad* as a heroic type and to bring to it our accumulated knowledge of the poet's tradition and age. For while such knowledge can be tremendously helpful and revealing once we have read the poem, it can also be misleading if we first read the *Iliad* in its reflected light. It is certainly true that the often repeated stock epithets—the "bright-eyed Athenes" and "rosy-fingered dawns"—were a part of the poet's working tradition and an enormous aid to the kind of oral composition he was expected to produce, but if, forearmed with such knowledge, we regard them *only* as inherited formulas, we are liable to miss the particular literary effects they have upon the poet's audience, ancient or modern: the individualization and particularization of characters in terms of specific traits, the expression of a pervasive and intuitively accepted faith in the permanence of the essential characters of men and in the abiding qualities of nature, the occasional irony which arises from a startling discrepancy between epithet and action, the suggestion of the importance of the daily rituals by which men live—all of these help to form the richly colored backdrop, the established world picture, before which the swift action of the poem takes place.

The *Iliad*, then, makes its first impression simply as story, as sheer narrative excitement, rather than as any particular type of literature for which preparation is demanded. It opens with an invocation, a prayer for inspiration, but this invocation is so presented that it hardly seems a prayer at all but, more to the poet's immediate purpose, a forceful presentation of theme. The "wrath of Achilles" and its effect, the suffering of the Achaeans, are the poet's stated subjects, and true to his word he plunges immediately and, more important, dramatically into the causes of the wrath. The poem does not begin, because it cannot dramatically afford to, with a lengthy exposition of the military situation or of the characters involved in the quarrel. There will be time for that later, but at the very outset we must observe (and not simply be told about), even without fully understanding it, the beginning of Achilles' wrath. Thus we have a few sentences devoted to the crisis at hand. An elderly priest of Apollo, Chryses, has come to King Agamemnon—and note how the epithet here serves as an introduction—to rescue his daughter Chryseis captured in war; immediately follows a highly charged scene in which Agamemnon, ignoring the expressed wishes of his army, summarily refuses, threatens, insults, and dismisses Chryses. Within a few lines Chryses has returned home and prayed for help to Apollo, who responds by sending a devastating nine-day plague upon the Achaeans.

In desperation Achilles, at the prompting of Here, does what Agamemnon is patently unwilling to do: he calls a full meeting of the assembly and in what seems to be a prearranged action calls upon the prophet Calchas to explain the cause of the plague. Calchas, having secured Achilles' protection from Agamemnon's spite, reveals Apollo's displeasure with the king. Agamemnon (ironically here "noble son of Atreus") turns first on Calchas, insulting him as a false prophet and refusing to return Chryseis. Achilles in turn takes up the argument, and immediately what purportedly began as a fact-finding inquiry becomes a bitter, public, mudslinging squabble between the noble sons of Atreus and Peleus. Achilles accuses Agamemnon of profiteering, of committing the whole of Greece to war to satisfy a personal vendetta, and of malingering, and threatens to withdraw from the field. Agamemnon in turn calls Achilles a brawler and a deserter and threatens to take from him his prize of war, the beautiful Briseis. The whole argument is punctuated by slanders of "unconscionable cur" and "drunken sot" and is saved from violence only by Athene's command that Achilles sheath his half-drawn sword. Despite the pleas of old Nestor, the council ends in a shambles, and Agamemnon, though agreeing to return Chryseis, makes good his threat by claiming Briseis.

In a matter of some three hundred lines the quarrel is over and the wrath has begun. It is a brilliant beginning—swift, dramatic, yet also suggestive in establishing the nature of the characters and the themes to come. Our initial sympathies lie with Achilles. Agamemnon is peremptory with Chryses; he obviously cares nothing for the opinions of either army or council; he ignores the sufferings of his army which his action has caused; he insults his soothsayer and dismisses his best warrior without a second thought. He is obviously in the wrong from start to finish and seems totally incapable of the leadership entrusted to him.

Achilles, on the other hand, is, in the beginning at least, calm and responsible. He obeys the prompting of the goddess and calls the council, probably in full knowledge that such action will infuriate Agamemnon. He carefully uses Calchas, and Calchas's position and authority, as a means of persuading Agamemnon to return Chryseis. True, he gives way to anger at Agamemnon's insults, but he obeys Athene's entreaties to sheath his sword and later politely turns Briseis over to Agamemnon's heralds, who are afraid even to approach him.

The argument, moreover, is broken by Athene's intervention and by Nestor's brief speech (brief at least for Nestor) urging that Achilles yield to Agamemnon's authority, on the grounds that it is god-given and embraces them all, and that Agamemnon refrain in turn from misusing that authority by taking Briseis. The old king's remarks, replete as usual with allusions to his own heroic past, define clearly the real issue which underlies the debate. For the disposition of Chryseis and Briseis cannot account for the bitterness of the quarrel or the enduring wrath that follows. The actual issue here is the authority of Agamemnon, its limits and responsibilities, and, more particularly, the proper relationship between individual warrior and group commander in a time of crisis. For Athene and Nestor are right: *aidos*, the mutual responsibility of leader and subordinate—the one to command intelligently, the other to obey unquestioningly—has indeed been violated on both sides.[1] The ultimate authority, however ill used, by divine commission lies with the king; Achilles has not the right to kill him nor should he act contentiously toward him. Paradoxically, however, the rebellious, individualistic Achilles has here shown much more concern for the welfare of the army than has Agamemnon, who by virtue of his office is entrusted with his men's safety, and so has some measure of right on his side. The poem thus begins not simply with an argument over a girl but with a complex question of the disposition and use of power and authority.

In short, aside from the use of epithets and speeches and actions of the gods, there is nothing in the opening of the *Iliad* to demonstrate that it conforms to the epic type as we have been taught to envision it. Instead of heroes performing superhuman deeds and playing out their fated, nationalistic roles, against a setting vast in scope, in "a style of sustained

4

elevation and grand simplicity,"[2] we have the vituperative tongue brawling of two most unheroic warriors engaged in a power struggle occasioned by the disposition of a slave girl. It is, as the undergraduates sense, an undignified spectacle at best and, honestly read, not at all what we should have expected of the archetype of the epic poem.

There is ample evidence, however, that this is Homer's calculated effect. For even without entering into a detailed discussion of the "Homeric question," the great debate over single or multiple authorship, one can demonstrate in the poem the kind of careful structure and thematic unification that one expects only in a poem composed by a single man; nowhere does literature, or any other art, demonstrate that either mere accumulation of traditional materials or corporate writing by a committee, however skilled,[3] can produce the unity of structure, theme, and characterization that the *Iliad* everywhere manifests. As C. M. Bowra has shown,[4] the first three books provide an introduction to the action by presenting the audience first with the wrath of Achilles, then with the first great war council of the Achaeans, and finally, in Book 3, with the Trojans and the first duel, that of Paris and Menelaus. The last three books complete the frame by treating the same three subjects in reverse order: Book 22 dramatizes the final duel, that of Achilles and Hector, and the lamentations of the Trojans; Book 23, the assembly of the Greeks at the funeral games of Patroclus; and Book 24, the appeasement of the wrath which began in Book 1. In Books 4–21, the Aristotelian middle, the account of the battle which ranges from the walls of Troy to the sea and back again is divided precisely into thirds by the two appearances of Achilles in Books 9 and 16.

Structure, moreover, here outlines and enforces the theme of authority with which the poem begins and with which it everywhere deals: we begin and end with the anger of Achilles, which is always kept in the thematic center of the poem. And though the structure demands that Achilles be absent from the battlefield in most of the poem, the effect of his absence is constantly felt in the waning fortunes of

5

the Achaean army as it is inexorably forced toward the beaches by the Trojan host, led by Hector. Moreover, by restricting our view of Achilles in the middle books to the scene in which he receives the embassy sent by Agamemnon to appease him and the one in which he grants Patroclus permission to wear his armor into battle, Homer is able to record precisely the stages of the hero's descent into *hubris;* he moves from righteous indignation to cold, unyielding fury to blind vanity, and finally, after the death of Patroclus, to bestiality.

Agamemnon, on the other hand, rises above his initial anger even as Achilles sinks beneath his. At first completely negligent of the welfare of his command, then tactless and peremptory in his efforts to urge his unit commanders into battle, after the first disastrous engagements he overcomes his impulse to give up the siege and responds to the advice of Nestor, admitting his "blind folly" and offering handsome amends to Achilles. Rebuffed by Achilles, he cannot sleep for fear that his army will be destroyed by the Trojans, who for the first time have dared to spend the night outside their impregnable walls and whose nearby campfires he can see. He personally leads the next morning's charge and is wounded, and following the death of Hector, at Achilles' request he orders wood gathered and Patroclus's funeral pyre prepared. We last see him yielding without demur to Achilles' decision to cancel the javelin-throwing contest and to award equal prizes to Agamemnon and Meriones, the only two contestants, though Agamemnon would certainly have won had the contest taken place. Agamemnon thus moves from selfish wrath and *hubris* to a sense of the responsibility of his office and an involvement in the war to a willingness to forgo a personal victory by accepting an equal share of the prize. While Briseis certainly is not to be equated with the new cauldron which Agamemnon receives, the king in his willingness to share with his men the spoils of war on equal terms displays at the end of the poem a far different concept of his office than he had held a month before.

What little is known of the antecedents of Agamemnon

and Achilles throws some light on their actions in the *Iliad* and hence on their roles as the chief representatives of authority and the individual. Here a few fundamental distinctions have to be made. It is clear that three kinds of source material were involved in the tradition of the Trojan War inherited by Homer: history—the remnants of actual persons, places, and events of the struggle, doubtless distorted by time but still in the main discernible, if not wholly accurate; legend—"primitive history . . . unconsciously transformed and simplified" beyond recognition by an accretion of folktales and wonders; and myth—the stories of the gods, ultimately derived from ritual—expressing in its simplest, though most illusive, form "primitive philosophy, . . . a series of attempts to understand the world, to explain life and death, fate and nature, gods and cults."[5] There was doubtless an actual Trojan War involving allied Greek forces, but in the centuries during which this unusual war was talked and sung about, its leaders and events became aggrandized by the natural tendency of primitive people to glorify and magnify their past heroes and history, and its causes and meaning came to be attributed to supernatural forces, the gods who continually oversee and in the long run control human history.

Unfortunately for the critic, the *Iliad* itself is, like *Beowulf,* our chief historical document for the period it represents, though indeed it contains even less "pure" history than does *Beowulf.*[6] Avoiding for the moment the tangle of technical arguments surrounding the time of composition, it seems clear that the *Iliad* was put into very nearly its present form in the eighth or ninth century B.C. and that its dramatic date, according to Greek tradition, is the late twelfth century, 1184 to be precise, some three to four hundred years earlier. There can be very little doubt that there was a siege of Troy; certainly the Greeks themselves regarded Homer's account as based on historical fact, and the archaeological work at Troy corroborates the possibility that an engagement took place somewhere around 1230.[7] On the other hand, our knowledge of Bronze Age chronology is so scanty as to make any speculation about the actual circumstances of the war extremely

7

risky. Since there are no early Greek accounts of the period, no one can say whether the war was caused by the abduction of a Greek queen, whether it resulted from the colonizing expeditions of the Aeolian tribes into Asia, or whether it was an attempt to break Troy's economic stranglehold on Greek shipping in the Hellespont.

Even so, some general conclusions about the period of the late twelfth century are possible. Whatever the relationship between Crete and the cities of the Greek mainland had been in earlier years, the Achaean stronghold of Mycenae had been from the time of the fall of Knossos in 1400, and probably for 150 years before, the greatest of the Greek kingdoms and remained so until well into the twelfth century. Her art, which shows during the early centuries of her dominance a strong Cretan influence, her tombs, fortifications, and palaces all evidence that Mycenae was the center of a great commercial empire which extended throughout the Peloponnesus and spread outward into Asia Minor and Cyprus and even into Egypt and Sicily. It was probably also the chief military power of the period, dominating its neighbors by "an elaborate system of gift-giving, which imposed reciprocal obligations without formal alliances or the necessity for a hierarchy of states."[8] As the tablets which have survived from Pylos and Mycenae show,[9] the social and economic life of the early Mycenaean period was organized minutely; the scrupulously kept accounts show a tightly controlled, though cumbrous, system of economic control over a vast area.

In time, however, a kind of decadence at home and aggressive restlessness abroad set in as Mycenae's trading empire was threatened by political and trading difficulties in Asia Minor and Egypt and by the decreasing wealth of Crete, from which she had long drawn a great part of her income. Egyptian and Hittite records dating from the late fourteenth century downward record a change in the relations between the Achaeans and their overseas neighbors. At first the allies of the Hittites, to whom they may have been related, against the Egyptians, by the middle thirteenth century Achaeans had become "sea raiders" fighting for the economic life of their empire against the Hittite colonies in Asia Minor as well as against Egypt. There are records of broken treaties and coastal raids, all evidencing the vigor with which the Mycenaeans pursued new trade routes and areas for colonization. In 1225 and 1194, together with other tribes, the Achaeans attacked Egypt unsuccessfully, but the cumulative effect of these campaigns was the destruction of the Hittite empire in Asia Minor and the beginning of political divisions among the Greeks. The wealth and influence of Mycenae apparently continued to decline until the great waves of Dorians in the twelfth century put an end to a civilization already crippled by economic failures, dynastic feuds and internal struggles, and a long and costly series of wars. The centuries following were in every way the "dark ages" of Greece.

It is during the last period of Mycenaean domination, the period of aggression and the struggle to survive, that Greek tradition placed Greece's "heroic age." Hesiod interposes an age of heroes between the age of bronze of early Mycenae and the prosaic age of iron in which he considered himself to live. The two great events of the heroic age, he tells us, were the sieges of Thebes and Troy. The Greeks themselves envisioned the heroic age as closing with the Doric invasions, and Homer's genealogies indicate that he thought of the period as encompassing some two hundred years, a period roughly coinciding with the restless, aggressive activities of the Achaeans, a time in which the whole Mediterranean world was marked by wars and confusion and the restless migration of its peoples.

It seems probable that while the epics of Homer reflect the warlike spirit of these later centuries, they occasionally in spirit if not in fact look back even further, to the tradition of the power and influence of early Mycenae. Certainly Homer had no accurate knowledge of life in the Mycenaean ages nor of the historical causes or conduct of the Trojan War; his picture of the period was likely a distorted one shaped by a long and probably at times a weak oral tradition. Almost every element in Homer is thus an amalgam. His

9

geography, his language, his poetic technique, his descriptions of armor, of battle procedures, architecture, customs, and beliefs—all derive both from the Ionic uses of the dark ages and of his own time and from the Mycenaean period, remnants of which were retained, though distorted, in the historical and poetic tradition which survived, probably through the descendants of Achaean refugees in Asia Minor. But the Achaean Confederacy is seen in the poem not as a desperate and decaying civilization, nor as one fighting for trade and colonization opportunities, but as the world's greatest established power in its heyday of unification and influence. The great catalog of ships demonstrates the range and might of its domain; the power of Agamemnon to keep a united expeditionary force in the field for ten years, the dominance of Mycenae in its organization.

The use of the term *Achaean* in Homer as a general name for the Greek force gathered at Troy is in itself puzzling. Certainly we are not to gather from it that there was ever anything resembling a single Mycenaean kingdom, much less a single people; but considered along with the Hittite records, the use of the term in Homer demonstrates that the Mycenaeans were indeed the dominant military group as well as the most prosperous people of the age. This fact throws considerable light on the position of Agamemnon and hence on his role in the poem. He is clearly commander in chief: he has the sole power to continue or abandon the siege, and the strategy and tactics of the war are his; he has in his power the disposition of the booty; he presides at council by virtue of the scepter; and he has, as Nestor says, a divine commission to command. But it is clearly the power to command rather than to rule absolutely. He may rebuke the stormy Achilles but not punish him, and although his decisions are final, he is constantly open to the criticisms of his officers and even of the common Thersites. His real power lies in his scepter rather than his person: Achilles can also use the scepter to call together a council, the purpose of which is to condemn an action of Agamemnon; and Odysseus can restrain the Greeks from leaving Troy only because he holds the scepter.

Agamemnon's position in the field as military commander of a conglomerate, though unified, expeditionary force seems to indicate the limits and degree of his authority as well as the place of Mycenae in the Achaean empire. Nestor clearly states that Agamemnon's authority is based on the wide extent of his kingdom. And not only does his kingdom, joined with that of Menelaus, encompass almost the whole Peloponnesus, but he is clearly the political overlord of some of his subordinates as well as their military superior. Yet, as the catalog makes clear, the Achaean leaders are for the most part kings in their own right and have merely delegated to Agamemnon the military authority necessary for efficient command. Like the Hittite commands of the same period, the Mycenaean military force was a confederacy of kings organized for efficient military action.

Such a position as that held by Agamemnon thus seems to be based on a confederacy of kings in the Mycenaean period rather than the disposition of the Ionian aristocracy in Homer's own time. Homer is portraying a historical reality, a portrait of military kingship drawn from the past. Whether or not an actual Agamemnon directed the operations at Troy is outside the sphere of debate; there is historical evidence neither for nor against his existence. Yet certain names appearing in the Hittite records may verify the existence of an Eteocles and an Atreus, and certainly some Achaean king directed the siege of Troy, whatever his name was.

To summarize briefly, the figure of Agamemnon is drawn from history, and his position reflects the extensive, though in some ways limited, power held by the Achaean commander in chief at Troy. The mixed nature of the authority delegated by the Achaean kings, moreover, does much to explain Agamemnon's dramatic role in the poem. According to the legend, the Greek rulers were called into service because of an agreement among them, made years before during their courtship of Helen, to protect the marriage of Menelaus and Helen should it be threatened. Having with some difficulty gathered the army at the port of Aulis, Agamemnon was unable to launch the expedition because of the enmity of the goddess Artemis, Apollo's sister. In desperation he agreed to sacrifice his daughter Iphigenia in return for favorable winds and so finally set sail.

But nine long years of frustration and deprivation have gone by. The Achaean kings, who were never eager to leave their homes to honor a long-forgotten, boyish agreement to protect Menelaus's wife, have become testy; a hoax designed by Agamemnon to test their loyalty reveals their eagerness to abandon the expedition. It is little wonder, therefore, that Agamemnon both resents and reacts hotly against any challenge to his authority, even one by the god Apollo. The general council of the Greeks clearly wishes him to return Chryseis; Achilles calls a meeting of the council without his consent; he is accused of personal cowardice; even the army soothsayer speaks against him. He is clearly in the wrong and probably knows it, but the circumstances are such that a proud man, pushed to the limits of his patience and fearful of his position, can react in no way except to bully his way through.

It should be remarked also that no question of romance or of a lady's honor is involved. Indeed Homer, especially in the *Odyssey*, creates a striking number of intelligent, sympathetic women, but Chryseis and Briseis have no real personalities in the poem, and it is clear that their captors care little for them. The captured girls are thus only the excuse for the quarrel among the chieftains. The real issue is *aidos*, the relationship between the commander in chief and his best warrior, and it is an issue which has presumably been simmering for a long time, needing only a catalyst to set it boiling.

Although Agamemnon reflects in his position, if not necessarily in his personality (which is almost purely the invention of Homer and/or an inherited tradition), a historical situation, Achilles does not seem to have been drawn at all from history but instead from myth. There is, in the first place, some confusion regarding his inclusion in the expedition at all.[10] He is not really an Achaean but is said to come from Phthia in Thessaly rather than from any of the Peloponnesian centers from which the other heroes are called. His people, the Myrmidons, are unknown to historians. He is thus to some degree an outlander, distinguished even by his speech from his compatriots. Throughout the *Iliad* he is a lonely figure; we never see him in close association with the other Greek leaders. He is, moreover, the only major hero to be killed during the war.

There are also an unusual number of tales associated with his birth and *enfance*. He is of semidivine origin; according to myth, his mother, Thetis, attempts to secure immortality for him by dipping him either in the river Styx or in fire. He is reared by Cheiron the centaur on Mount Pelion, and his weapons and horses are miraculous. He is, moreover, doomed either to live a long, though pedestrian, life or to fall in glory at Troy.

His actions and powers also are different not only in degree but also in kind from those of the other heroes: his armor is forged by the god Hephaestus; a magical fire blazes about his head on the eve of battle; in his ire he fights the swollen Xanthus. Homer throws about Achilles, as about none of the other characters, an aura of the superhuman and the mythical. Even the gods seem to respect and shun him; unlike the other heroes, he is free from their tricks and deceits.

Scholars have pointed out a number of similarities between the careers of Achilles and Siegfried,[11] those of Achilles and Cuchulain,[12] and those of the Greek hero and Gilgamesh.[13] Like Achilles, Siegfried is entrusted to an outsider, the dwarf Regin, to be reared and is given a magical bath, in dragon's blood, to gain invulnerability. He inherits a miraculous sword, as Achilles does a spear, from his father, and he too rides a horse which has supernatural powers. Cuchulain's horses, like Achilles', shed tears of grief, and the Irish hero also possesses a magical spear and is surrounded in battle by a supernatural aura. As T. L. Webster points out, the relationship between Gilgamesh and his companion Enkidu is very like that of Achilles and Patroclus, especially in the violent grief which the heroes show for the death of their companions; and there is a remarkable similarity between the heroes in scenes in which their mothers appeal to the gods for help.

13

While there is little point in assigning to the tales of these heroes a common origin, it does seem at least plausible to conjecture that they stem from the same type of source—myth rather than history, or history enlarged by legend.

The origins of these four heroes, moreover, have at least one factor in common: they all seem to be intimately associated with the sun gods of the mythic traditions from which they are derived. Although solar myth is in general discredit today,[14] the solar mythologists were almost certainly correct in seeing Siegfried's penetration of the magic fire to awaken the sleeping Brunhild as a symbolization of the sun awakening the sleeping dawn. Among the traditions associated with Cuchulain, one maintains that he never rose later than the sun and another that "the intense heat generated by his body melted the snow round him for thirty feet." His head is surrounded by "a diadem of gold," his shining, yellow hair; and his contortions suggest "the transformation of the sun-god into the fire-shooting thunder cloud."[15] It may well be that the signs of the Zodiac, through which the sun runs its yearly course, "gradually evolved in Babylonia from the twelve incidents in the life-story of the hero Gilgamesh."[16] Greek mythology also bears witness to the importance of solar myth in the history of religion: "Helias, Kronos, Zeus, Apollo, Phaethon, Talus, Hercules, Phoebus, Admetus, Ixion, Aesculapius, Hyperion, Hades, Ares, Hippolytus, Janus, all had their solar aspects,"[17] and our post-Frazerian habit of thinking only in terms of vegetation myths should not obscure the awe in which primitive man held the sun, and the central place of the sun in his religion.

The fact that Achilles seems descended from a solar myth —though he may well have connections with other myths as well—helps to explain his role in the *Iliad,* though I should be unwilling to interpret the whole poem, or even any single episode in it, as being mythical, as distinct from historical or legendary, in origin or conception. Certainly, however, his unrelenting fury and the aura which surrounds his head seem vestiges of his mythic past, as does his appearance at dawn on the last day of battle after his long sojourn in his tent. I would not insist on this point, but it may well be that Achilles' retreat in isolation reflects also, at least in part, the withdrawal-return pattern which is an essential part of the myth of the questing hero.[18] For although most of the familiar stages in the withdrawal-return—the call to adventure, the crossing of the threshold, etc.—are not to be found in the *Iliad,* Achilles does indeed return to his people to bring victory out of defeat.

But my central point is that the figure of Achilles is the only one derived from myth and that his mythic origin explains his individuality, his isolation from others and from their common cause. Never after the initial quarrel with Agamemnon does he exhibit the slightest interest in an Achaean victory. He is perfectly willing, therefore, to sacrifice the whole mission to justify his own position and to salve the wound of a personal assault. All the efforts of Odysseus and Phoenix to appeal to his sense of duty or his responsibility to their common cause fail simply because he has no conception of such a role. When he finally does emerge, it is to avenge a personal wrong, the death of Patroclus, and even here he fights as an individual; his killing of Hector is prompted not by Hector's position as leader of the enemy forces but by the fact that Hector killed Patroclus. When at last his fury is abated and his wrath assuaged, it is not because he realizes that his actions have been irresponsible and his brutality unreasonable but because Priam's grief moves him to think of his own father and his father's sorrows.

Thus the *Iliad* poses as antagonists king and captain: the historical Agamemnon, whose sense of the responsibility of leadership steadily grows until it overcomes the egotism and personal pride that originally inspired his quarrel with Achilles; and the mythical Achilles, whom fury and pride send raving into alienation until he becomes more beast than man. The other characters of the poem, moreover, illuminate various aspects of this central clash in authority. As C. M. Bowra has pointed out, the minor characters tend to "fall into two classes, the soldiers and the statesmen. In the first class are Aias, Diomedes, and Menelaus, and in the second are Nestor and Odysseus."[19] Like Achilles, Aias and Diomedes are essentially individualistic warriors, fierce and aggressive in combat; neither has any use for the councils of the wise. Diomedes, in fact, will not accept Agamemnon's grief-stricken decision to abandon the siege and deplores Agamemnon's having humbled himself in attempting to make amends to Achilles.

But neither Aias nor Diomedes can match Achilles. Aias is compared by Homer to both a lion and an ass; he has a stubborn natural courage, but he is essentially slow-witted, a great, hulking brute whose ultimate fate is frustration, dumb rage, and suicide. He thus differs from Achilles, whose intelligence immediately pierces Priam's flattery. Diomedes has a good deal of Achilles' dash and brilliance in the field, but he lacks the fury that makes Achilles "godlike" in battle. The scene in which Diomedes and Glaucus courteously exchange armor on the battlefield sharply contrasts with Achilles' refusal to spare the unarmed and suppliant Lycaon. Both Aias and Diomedes, however, help to define the essential quality that sets Achilles apart from the others: an unswerving and unalterable faith in the rightness of his own conduct, a prideful self-assurance capable of destroying an army for the sake of personal honor.

The true foil to Achilles is, of course, Hector, his Trojan counterpart and, at least to modern readers, the most sympathetic of the heroes. Unlike Achilles he fights only to protect his home and country, and his prowess and heroism stem from necessity rather than, as with Achilles, the fury of personal insult. The famous scenes with Andromache show him at his best, kind and loving, yet thoroughly responsible, a conscientious soldier and a wise leader. Yet the fire of the gods never burns about his head, nor in the end can he understand the nature of the man whose ire he has incurred. He decides to press the Trojans' hard-won military advantage by opposing Achilles and later to stand alone against his fury. But at the sight of Achilles brandishing the spear of Pelion, his armor glowing "like a blazing fire or the rising sun, he no longer had the heart to stand his ground; he left

the gate, and ran away in terror."[20] In the end Hector is
duped by Athene into fighting and dies charging into Achilles'
lance. Deliberate courage and prowess and a cause to defend
have failed to stand against the wrath of the godlike Achilles.

The characters of Nestor and Odysseus throw light in
much the same way upon that of Agamemnon. For if Agamemnon struggles to understand the nature of authority and
command, Nestor is surely past understanding it. A man of
great experience, he has come to live only in the past and its
glories, and therefore his experience is of little use to the
Greeks. His advice is nearly always ineffective and at times
almost disastrous. It is he who on the basis of a false dream
counsels the building of the wall, which soon crumbles under
the Trojan assault, without offering the necessary sacrifices
to Poseidon. The futile embassy to Achilles is his idea as is
the plan to have Patroclus appear on the battlefield dressed
in Achilles' armor. In Nestor Homer portrays the uselessness
of mere experience as a basis for authority and wise decision,
and though Nestor can in his interminable yarns suggest a
heroic standard of conduct, the appeals to valor by the high-
spirited Diomedes are much more effective in rallying the
army.

Odysseus, on the other hand, is (in the *Iliad*, at least)
so totally involved in the affairs of the moment that he lacks
the breadth of judgment great authority demands. He oper-
ates always at the level of device and stratagem and is thus
always the man called upon to deal with the immediate problem by the most practicable means. He can be trusted to return Chryseis to her father with perfect tact; he manages to
cope with the panic that follows Agamemnon's announcement that the army will embark for home; he can worm information from the unsuspecting Dolon; he wins the wres-
tling contest with Aias by a trick; and he even talks the
bloodthirsty Achilles into allowing his soldiers to eat before
battle. But he fails in the greatest, the only crucial mission
assigned him: he cannot dent Achilles' determination to refrain from battle; his subtlest arguments cannot match
Achilles' prideful determination. He is in every way a man of

the greatest intelligence and charm, but he lacks Agamemnon's stature and honesty and, ultimately, his sense of the responsibilities of power.

The gods also reflect, in their eternal bickering, the theme of the nature of authority that so occupies the heroes below. Zeus rules by sheer power rather than intelligence and is reduced all too often to shouting and threatening. The other gods, wary of his thunderbolts, must take advantage of their father in whatever devious ways they can: Here by nagging and eventually by seduction, Athene by argument, Aphrodite by flattery, Thetis (not even a close relative) by wheedling. Whatever Homer may have thought of the gods, it is clear that they present no proper model for government among men.

Because of the scantiness of biographical and historical information, it is difficult to ascertain with any hope of exactitude Homer's ultimate purposes in the poem. He almost certainly lived in the late ninth or early eighth century, apparently in Ionia in Asia Minor, and was thoroughly trained in the usages of formulaic poetry. He was, moreover, an inheritor of a long tradition of lays concerning the Trojan War, a tradition which he might well fabricate into a single brilliantly conceived and executed poem but which he could not basically change. The major causes, events, and characters of the tradition were beyond alteration; similarly, one could not today write a poem, however heroic, in which the South won the Civil War and Lincoln appeared as a drunken scoundrel. But Homer, by selection and emphasis, might well use his tradition to shape a theme. He might not alter a received character, but he might, by the addition of detail, shape that character to fit his own purpose.[21]

It is this sense of purpose that everywhere distinguishes the *Iliad* from the imitations and continuations of the so-called epic cycle that follow it. Obviously Homer did not recount the ancient stories simply for their own sakes; in fact he leaves out the most exciting among them, that of the Trojan Horse. Nor are they told historically; the full chronology of the war is not only ignored but often, as in the engagement of Menelaus and Paris in Book 3, actually violated.[22] Nor are they told, as men often tell stories of the past, either reminiscently or, despite Robert Graves's interpretation, satirically;[23] the poet is neither a Nestor nor a Mark Twain.

Some help in determining Homer's attitude toward the past, and hence in defining his purpose, may be gleaned from the bits of history that have come down to us. The Greek world of Homer's own time was emerging from over two hundred years of civil chaos and cultural disruption, the so-called dark ages. Undeniably, however, the Ionian colonies had prospered as a result of the new trade and maritime ventures that followed the dark ages, and by Homer's time they must have enjoyed considerable social stability. More important, Ionia had by then completed, as had most of the Greek kingdoms, the shift from a monarchic to an aristocratic and federal form of government, a change caused primarily by the shift in population from the land to well-defined cities, what are later to emerge as the great city-states of the golden ages. These new aristocratic republics such as that under which Homer must have lived were governed for the most part efficiently, though rather narrowly. The governing class was trained in the business of ruling, and they passed their knowledge and skill along from generation to generation.

There is little doubt that the new form of government rescued the Greek cities from the anarchy and poverty which followed the collapse of the Mycenaean empire. Colonization began anew throughout the Aegean area and eventually beyond, and under the careful direction of the new republics it became systematic and profitable. The colonies had to be supplied both with agricultural goods such as wool and with manufactured articles and so provided the republics with new markets as well as sources of raw materials. The new age might well have been, as Hesiod complained, an age of iron in which the practices of the ages of silver and gold had fallen into disuse, but it also created social conditions in which a poetry celebrating the glories of those former ages might be composed; furthermore, it provided through its commerce with Phoenicia an instrument, the alphabet, which could preserve those glories forever.

I would maintain that Homer, looking back from the point of view of a romanticized tradition, saw the great legend of the Trojan War not merely, like Hesiod, as the record of an adventurous and golden time; more important, he saw it as raw material for a commentary on the life of both ages, gold and iron alike, and on the great problem common to both—the individual's relation to the state, and the values involved in the conflict between ruler and ruled, between loyalty to the state and the rights of the individual.

To frame this great commentary Homer selected from the oral tradition of history and legend and myth which had kept alive the memory of the war at Troy a single incident, the quarrel of Agamemnon and Achilles, and by arrangement and emphasis built into his account of that incident all his reflections upon his own time and the heroic past. Not that the poem is a personal judgment and commentary in the sense that a Romantic poem is, for Homer observes scrupulously the objectivity of the great classical artist. He narrates and shapes the action, but he never imposes his own voice on it. To do so would have been to sacrifice universality and to reduce the poem to something less than heroic in scope. But a judgment is there, nevertheless, implicit in the actions and speeches of the characters and in the development of the conflict between the two great antagonists.

We too often read the *Iliad* as though it were only an *Achilliad,* as though Achilles were the only person of interest. He is, as I have said, the thematic center of the poem; everything depends upon his actions. Yet opposed to him stands the rest of the *dramatis personae,* the Greek force led by Agamemnon. One man thus stands against a whole state, and by an odd whim of destiny this person holds in his hands the fate of the nation. Victory or defeat is his to give, and for a few days in the midst of a raging battle the representatives of state and the individual stand opposed.

The resolution of this opposition is the substance of the *Iliad.* Agamemnon must learn that authority entails responsibility, that he cannot rule by prideful whim, and that he cannot jeopardize the safety of his command or the success of his expedition merely to demonstrate publicly the extent of his power. In the end his values are those of the organization which he both commands and serves. If in order to assure the success of the group he must conquer his natural inclination to despair, subdue his haughty spirit and imperious attitude, humble himself before his subordinate, and even refuse to snatch a trivial moment of glory in the javelin-throwing contest, then these things he must do. Originally drawn from history, he must in the poem develop within himself a sense of history and of his place in it. The greatest values of the leader in any age, golden or iron, are those of responsibility and loyalty to his cause and to his command.

Opposed to these values are those of Achilles—personal honor and the integrity of the individual. At first identified with and subject to the common welfare, Achilles' honor, once slighted (over however trivial a matter), turns sour; growing like a tumor within the hero, it becomes *hubris* and comes to dominate his personality. His mythic origins are far older than the historical origins of the king; like the sun, he rules alone, subject in his blazing pride to no laws beyond his own, loyal only to the dictates of his own honor. But unchecked *hubris* can lead only to irresponsibility and disaster. Achilles' motives in allowing Patroclus to appear in his armor are essentially egocentric. In granting permission to Patroclus he reiterates, rather pathetically now, his long list of grievances, expresses his delight at the Trojan victories, and cautions Patroclus not to perform too brilliantly lest he cheapen his own eventual reappearance as ultimate savior of the Greek force. In short he is delighted at the opportunity to demonstrate, as Patroclus has suggested, that his armor alone can rout the Trojan host.

After the death of Patroclus Achilles' high-minded *hubris* becomes simply animal rage and his atrocities mount; he kills indiscriminately everyone who opposes him on the battlefield, mutilates the dead body of Hector, and burns twelve young Trojans on Patroclus's pyre. But just before he begins the bloodbath which will culminate in Hector's death, he becomes reconciled with Agamemnon; admits his error in withdrawing from the common effort, an action from which only Hector and the Trojans profited; and urges that Agamemnon order an attack. Agamemnon, insisting that the whole army listen, apologizes in turn and the breach is healed. However, Achilles' wrath, now turned upon the Trojans, continues until the visit of Priam, and it is clear from his rebuffs of Priam's attempts at flattery that his ire still lies very close to the surface.

Homer thus reaches no solution to the dilemma he has faced. Agamemnon, it is true, comes to understand his kingly responsibility, but in doing so he must sacrifice the pride and personal integrity that so distinguishes Achilles. Achilles, on the other hand, maintains the sense of honor and fierce individualism that mark the hero, but they lead only to tragedy and in the end to quiet resignation. Yet paradoxically, Agamemnon appears at his best in apologizing publicly to Achilles and in graciously agreeing to share the prize with Meriones —in short, when he is most humble and least heroic; and Achilles is most impressive when, at the height of his ungoverned rage, he stands upon the beach, Athene's light upon his head, and three times howls his defiance at the Trojans.

Nearly everyone has remarked upon Homer's sense of the futility and waste of war, but no one has seriously questioned his approval of what are usually designated as the chief values of the heroic age: a sense of honor so great that it cannot brook the slightest affront; loyalty and fidelity to one's comrades—what is later to be called the *comitatus* code; and generosity.[24] Yet it is obvious that in the *Iliad* these heroic values are contradictory. What indeed happens when the value of honor crosses that of loyalty, when the rights of the individual conflict with those of society? Both values are rightful parts of the heroic code; because Hector and Diomedes can observe both, they are the most admirable of the warriors. Yet these values do conflict, and it is in their opposition that one finds, I think, the real strength of heroic literature. For all their bravery and intelligence, Hector and Diomedes cannot reach the glorious heights which Achilles reaches in his raging, wrongheaded, but nonetheless heroic, fury. Conscious always of the fate which hangs over him, he is willing to sacrifice his own welfare and that of his companions to satisfy a point of honor. And Agamemnon, despite his almost schizophrenic moodiness and, in the end, his most unheroic humility, is always a more responsible, because more concerned, leader than either the garrulous Nestor or the crafty Odysseus. The very opposite of Achilles, Agamemnon is willing to reduce himself to what must seem to be, by heroic standards, abject obsequiousness in order to further the Greek cause which he leads and for which he is responsible.

I would maintain that this carefully sustained ambivalence represents the considered point of view of a writer, perhaps the wisest who ever lived, looking back from a highly structured commercial society toward a heroic age—to use David Riesman's terms, from an other-directed to an inner-directed society. That Homer recognizes the virtues of the former age is certain; his love of its dignity and strength is apparent in every line. But that does not mean that "this code of behavior seems to have been accepted by Homer without limitations."[25] Certainly the more prosaic values of the newer age are everywhere seen to balance the excesses of the older code. Both individual heroism and corporate authority are ideals worthy to be upheld, but they may well conflict and their opposition may bring about the destruction of both the individual and his society. Homer is able to view the great Bronze Age heroes with the rationalism and objectivity of a man who lives just outside the era of which he writes and who is able because of an unusual critical intelligence to escape its sentimental appeal.

Something of this outlook can be seen in the theology of the poem. Homer's treatment of the gods seems to reflect a transitional stage in the development of Greek religion, one that was perhaps peculiar to Ionia.[26] There is certainly very little resembling the ancient rituals and totems of the early Minoan-Mycenaean deities[27] and no hint of the cults of

Orpheus and Dionysus which would later become dominant. The migration to Ionia had freed the old gods from any attachments to particular shrines on the mainland and so had vastly simplified the theology as well as the system of the old religion. And as C. M. Bowra says, a new rationalism, "essentially aristocratic and careless,"[28] had resulted in a critical attitude toward the old gods, an outlook that made possible Homer's satiric, playful treatment of the Olympians.

Yet there is far more in Homer's use of theology than simply a spirit of rationalism playing upon a set of archaic concepts, for there are in the *Iliad* powers equal to and even more powerful than Zeus and Poseidon. First are the abstractions, partially personified as minor deities, of the passions— Blind Folly (*ate*), Fear (*phobos* and *deimos*), Strife (*eris*), and Turmoil (*kudoimos*)—that control man in his hours of crisis. We should perhaps call them "animal instincts" or even the id; later Greeks surely associated them with man's unruly animal spirit. Strife, we remember, tossed the golden apple of jealousy and discord upon the table at the wedding of Peleus and Thetis and so set in motion the train of events leading to the Trojan War. Fear and Strife are said to be present on the battlefield along with Ares and Athene, and Strife and Turmoil are personified as bloody figures on Achilles' shield. More important, Achilles is seen as the victim of both Strife and Folly: Agamemnon tells him that he loves Strife, and Phoenix accuses him of having been overcome by Folly and of having neglected to pray to Zeus for deliverance from her terrible ravages. In time, of course, Blind Folly does exact her toll. Achilles, filled with the *hubris* that comes from Folly, is responsible for the death of Patroclus; his indulgence of his passions leads to disaster and almost to the destruction of his personality.

One enemy against which both Achilles and Agamemnon contend, then, is that tendency to give way to those passions, *hubris* and *ate*, Pride and Folly, which debilitate reason; indeed it would seem that Homer creates a race of minor deities precisely to exemplify such passions. The traditional gods are, of course, often used in much the same way—

Helen is the slave of her own sensuality as personified by Aphrodite; warriors in battle are said to be under the control of the bloodthirsty Ares—but the very fact that Homer saw fit to personify Folly seems to indicate that he wished to emphasize strongly the essentially moral and psychological nature of Agamemnon's and Achilles' struggles with their own natures and that he could find among the figures of the inherited gods no fit representatives of such a struggle. For whatever qualities they represent—power, wisdom, beauty—the major gods as Homer received them are essentially amoral. They live in trickery and deceit, using men as pawns in their own struggles for power on Olympus.

Homer reinforces the moral nature of the poem by yet another means, also connected with his use of the gods. It is clear, both in the *Iliad* and in Greek mythology itself, that the Olympians are subject to powers older and more powerful than they, chiefly the Moerae, or Fates, and Themis, or Order. The three Fates are usually said to have been begotten by Erebus on Night long before the reign of Zeus, but according to some Greek interpretations of the myth they are "the parthenogenous daughters of the Great Goddess Necessity, against whom not even the gods contend."[29] Themis the titaness was a part of the original created order, appointed by Eurynome, the "goddess of all things,"[30] to help rule the planet Jupiter. Both the Fates and Order are connected, moreover, with the story of the downfall of Troy. Hector attributes his approaching death to Fate, and he is kept by Fate outside the Scaean Gate to meet Achilles. Zeus himself twice allows the scales of Fate to decide the day's battles, and the same scales seal the doom of Hector. Many times also Zeus is mentioned by the principals not simply as the ruler of Olympus, his usual role, but as the agent of destiny; Helen, Achilles, and Priam all attribute their fates to him.

While Themis does not appear in the poem, it was to avert her prophecy, that Thetis would bear a child greater than its father, that Zeus arranged the marriage of the sea nymph to Peleus; indeed Themis at one time was the chief oracle of Delphi. She is twice invoked along with Zeus in the *Odyssey*. Robert Graves states that from her Zeus "derived his judicial authority"[31] and that along with Zeus she caused the destruction of Troy.[32] Her role in Greek myth is perhaps best described by Graves's statement that she represents the "female sense of orderliness" as opposed to "the restless and arbitrary male will," Zeus.[33]

I would maintain that these two forces, Fate and Order, are constantly present in the poem; that they represent moral and ethical forces which the Olympian gods, because of their traditional amorality, cannot; and that they, and not the Olympians, direct the destinies of heroes and nations. Again, there can be little doubt that the *Iliad* is essentially a moral poem: Agamemnon grows in stature and Achilles shrinks because the one by means of internal struggle overcomes his first *hubris* and the other, yielding to *ate,* succumbs to it. Troy, too, by protecting Paris and thereby condoning his immoral actions, the violation of Menelaus's hospitality and the abduction of Helen, is guilty of both *ate* and *hubris* and so must bear the punishment of a moral universe. Though the gods may bicker and squabble and men may fancy that they can avoid the consequences of their actions, Fate and Order, necessity and justice, reign; and every morning's rosy-fingered dawn rising above the lifegiving sea testifies to their eternal watch over Homer's universe.

In short I think Homer to be far closer in thought to Aeschylus than to Hesiod. True, he has not quite reached the point of consciously and systematically identifying Zeus with the principle of justice that rules the universe (though he occasionally does so), but through his use of gods, personified passions, and the powers of Fate and Order, he is able to construct a complete image of man at war with his fellow men, with himself, and with the moral forces of the universe whose laws he may momentarily evade but must eventually recognize and acknowledge.

Agamemnon, Achilles, Helen, and Priam are all aware that their ends are predetermined and immutable. But all are conscious that driven by passion, they must at least to some degree assume "the burden of necessity": Agamemnon sacrifices Iphigenia; Achilles chooses to hasten his death by participating in the war, specifically by driving into the Trojan host, though Xanthus has warned him against doing so; Helen yields to Paris; Priam shields the lovers and begs Hector to save Troy, though he knows the city is doomed. Because there is room in the Homeric scheme of things for both free will and destiny, man is able to a degree to be the architect of his own fate: he may or may not sacrifice his daughter, or fight at Troy, or yield to Paris, or protect Helen. Yet having done so, he cannot escape the consequences of his action, the destiny that Fate imposes on him. Nevertheless, he is still free, even knowing his fate (though not its exact terms), to respond to it as he will. He may simply try to live it down, to wear it out by the practice of virtue as do Agamemnon, Helen, and Priam. Or he may heroically defy it, as does Achilles. In either case, however, despite all the maneuvering of the gods and the evasions and heroism of men, Order and Fate prevail.

The religious structure of the poem, like the political, thus contains a fusion of old and new values. Homer uses the traditional figures of the gods, along with other personifications, to delineate the passions and motives of men in crisis. To this older, amoralistic theology, however, he adds, again through the use of already established deities, the concept of an ordered and moral universe which both governs and judges the actions of men, a universal order which startlingly resembles that described hundreds of years later by Aeschylus in the *Agamemnon*.

In this discussion of the *Iliad* I have largely avoided references to other works of heroic literature, though many parallels will have occurred to the reader. Yet even without the corroboration which such comparisons would have brought, it is possible to frame as hypotheses for the next chapters a few general statements based on this study of the *Iliad*, which as the first and probably the major heroic work in the western tradition should be the source of all such generalizations. Thus while my observations do not correspond with the traditional handbook statements describing heroic literature, they nevertheless have behind them the authority of the *Iliad,* if not of later commentators.

First, there is a considerable time lapse between the event and the heroic work, a period in which history, legend, and myth become inextricably mixed within an oral tradition.

Second, the work demonstrates a well-defined structure and a sense of purpose that suggest the hand of a single author who is both selecting and organizing the many strands of the diffuse tradition into a single thematic unit.

Third, the work involves a struggle between the corporate authority and the individual, each of which is seen to have both faults and virtues. Through this opposition the poet is examining the individualistic values of an older, traditionally a more "heroic," age along with the corporate values of the more systematic age in which he lives, the strong sense of personal honor of the first side by side with the duties of co-operation and the loyalty of the second.

Fourth, the figure of the king, who represents authority, tends to have its origins in history, while that of the hero, whose individualistic values are opposed to those of the king, tends to be derived from myth.

Fifth, the theology of the poem represents an amalgamation of the older, amoral, polytheistic myth structure with the more sophisticated notion of man's struggle with his passions within the framework of a just and moral universal order.

Such a list does not even roughly coincide with the usual catalog of epic characteristics and conventions, and to these differences we shall return. But it will, I hope, draw attention to one basic fact, that this first great poem of the western literary tradition encompasses within its vast thematic range the central concerns of western man—his relationship to self, state, nature, and God. In the end it is impossible to say what the *Iliad* is *only* about or what conclusions it reaches. After the passion and turmoil of open warfare and personal conflict, the poem ends quietly. An uneasy truce reigns on the battlefield; Achilles is grieving, quietly now, over the death of Patroclus; and the last hope of Troy is buried in a golden chest as "dawn came once more, lighting the East with rosy hands."[34]

When that dawn rises again in Homer, it will reveal a different scene, a lone sailor painfully making his way homeward after ten years of wandering.

CHAPTER TWO

The Odyssey

The *Odyssey* begins, as does the *Iliad*, with a general statement of theme and a plea, probably traditional, for assistance from the Muse:

> The hero of the tale which I beg the Muse to help me tell is that resourceful man who roamed the wide world after he had sacked the holy citadel of Troy. He saw the cities of many peoples and he learnt their ways. He suffered many hardships on the high seas in his struggles to preserve his life and bring his comrades home. But he failed to save those comrades, in spite of all his efforts. It was their own sin that brought them to their doom, for in their folly they devoured the oxen of Hyperion the Sun, and the god saw to it that they should never return. This is the tale I pray the divine Muse to unfold to us. Begin it, goddess, at whatever point you will.[1]

Like the opening of the *Iliad*, which identifies the wrath of Achilles as the unifying theme of the poem, this beginning immediately emphasizes the centrality of the wanderings of Odysseus to the *Odyssey*. Strangely enough, however, it says nothing of what the structure of the poem itself leads us to expect Homer's major theme to be—the homecoming of the hero. After all, twelve of the twenty-four books of the poem deal with Odysseus's adventures after he has landed in Ithaca, four with the quest of Telemachus for his father, and four with the hero's short journey to and reception at Phaeacia; only four books are given over to the famous wanderings to which Homer obviously alludes in the proem and on which he seems to place his thematic emphasis. There seems to be, therefore, a basic discrepancy between his announced theme and the total effect of the poem.

It has become almost customary in modern discussions of the *Odyssey* to concentrate upon Odysseus's role as the returning king and to ignore as vestigial remains of folktales and myths the adventures of the hero among his monstrous foes. Yet it is clear from the proem that Homer felt the wanderings to be important, however much he emphasized the establishment of peace in Ithaca by means of structure and arrangement within the poem. One may, of course, dismiss the proem (he cannot very well disregard the structure and emphasis of the poem as a whole) as a crude preliminary statement of purpose which Homer later modified but did not bother to revise. And there is no reason, as Howard W. Clarke says, "why a proem should have to serve as a table of contents."[2] Yet a writer as careful as Homer can never be presumed to nod, especially on a matter as crucial as the announcement of the theme of a long and complex poem. It may well be, therefore, that there is method here; Homer may have wished to serve notice in advance that although the structure and balance of the poem will make clear the importance of Odysseus's homecoming, the fabulous adventures are equally an integral part of the total poem and hence of its theme, despite the relatively small space devoted to them.

It is noteworthy that Homer views the wanderings of Odysseus not simply as a disconnected series of adventures but as an educational process; the hero "saw the cities of many peoples and he learnt their ways," we are told. Again, this is not quite what, having read the poem, we should have expected Homer to say in the proem. Aside from Troy, where the ten-year journey begins, and Ithaca, where it ends, Odysseus visits only two cities—Ismarus, the home of the Cicones, and the capital city of the Phaeacians on Scherie. Significantly, however, these two cities mark the beginning and end of the wanderings, Ismarus being the site of Odysseus's first adventure after leaving Troy, and Phaeacia his last stop before his arrival at Ithaca.

Again, it may be that in the proem Homer wishes to identify a major theme which the structure of the poem will not permit him to emphasize. I think we are to see the wanderings not only as important thematically, but also as contributing to the development of Odysseus's character.

The rest of the proem is devoted to a matter which, superficially at least, receives almost no emphasis within the poem—Odysseus's efforts to bring his comrades home—a matter, Homer intimates, as important to the hero as the preservation of his own life. As Howard W. Clarke says, "It is difficult to think very long or very hard about Odysseus' comrades."[3] They are for the most part faceless nonentities who are gradually killed off during the long voyage home; certainly they are of no importance whatsoever to plot or structure. Yet Homer's statement here seems to indicate that they and their fate are of considerable importance to the major theme.

At this point Homer also points with considerable emphasis to the reason for the deaths of Odysseus's sailors. Despite Odysseus's efforts to save them, the poet says, they insisted in their folly on devouring the oxen of Hyperion and so "the god saw to it that they should never return." Yet only a small remnant of Odysseus's original crew are actually destroyed on Hyperion's island. Having begun the journey with twelve ships, Odysseus loses six warriors from each ship at Ismarus, six men to Polyphemus, eleven ships with their crews to the Laestrygonians, poor Elpenor on Circe's island, six men to Scylla, and the rest in the storm that Zeus sends as a punishment for the crew's slaughter of Hyperion's cattle. The responsibility for these losses varies: Odysseus, though responsible for the sacking of Ismarus, blames his defeat there on the greed of his sailors. His capture by Polyphemus is, however, clearly his own fault, as he admits. The great loss to the Laestrygonians is really no one's fault, unless Odysseus's precaution in anchoring his own ship outside the harbor indicates that the captains of the other eleven vessels took it upon themselves to ignore some signs of danger which their commander noted; however, the eleven captains certainly cannot be said to have incurred willfully the disaster that overtook them. Elpenor's death is his own fault and, according to Circe, the loss of six men to Scylla was inevitable. Thus only the losses to the Cicones and the sinking of Odysseus's last vessel can be attributed to the folly of which Homer specifically accuses the crew in the proem.

On the other hand, it may well be that Homer is speaking here only of the greed that overcame the sailors when they slaughtered the cattle of the sun and not at all of the other losses that Odysseus suffers. He may thus be indicating that only the final loss of men and ships was due to the folly of the crew and that however prideful and negligent Odysseus might have been in blinding Polyphemus, hence incurring the wrath of Poseidon, in the end he regained his sense of responsibility but "failed to save those comrades, in spite of all his efforts."

"This," then, the fabulous wanderings of Odysseus, "is the tale [Homer prays] the divine Muse to unfold to us," and he begs the goddess to begin it "at whatever point [she] will." She chooses, oddly enough, to begin with Odysseus marooned on Calypso's island, having passed through most of his adventures; after a brief council of the gods she launches into the long account of Telemachus's search for his father, returns four books later to the announced topic, the wanderings of the hero, only to abandon it after another four books to devote the bulk of the poem to a topic not even touched on in the proem—the return of the king and the scouring of Ithaca.

A brief look at the plan of the *Odyssey* will help to clarify Homer's intentions. Unlike the *Iliad,* which falls into a three-book beginning, a three-book conclusion, and an eighteen-book middle punctuated by the two appearances of Achilles, the *Odyssey* breaks squarely in half, the first twelve books dealing with the pre-Ithacan adventures of the hero and the last twelve directly with his conquest of the suitors on Ithaca. Each half of the book in turn breaks down into three groups of four books each: Books 1–4, the so-called *Telemacheia;* Books 5–8, the journey of Odysseus from Ogygia to Phaeacia and his reception there; Books 9–12, the fabulous adventures; Books 13–16, the trip from Phaeacia to Ithaca and Odysseus's meetings there with Eumaeus and Telemachus; Books 17–20, the journey to the palace and the preparations there for the coming battle; Books 21–24, the killing of the suitors and the reestablishment of Odysseus as king. Each half of the poem has its own appropriate general structure: the first twelve books are episodic, the last twelve dramatic and climactic. Also indicative of a planned structure is the fact that each four-book unit, except of course the last, revolves about a journey, or rather a clearly defined stage in the quest of Odysseus.

I see in the structure of the poem as a whole, then, no indication whatsoever that Homer changed his mind about his intentions at any point during the process of composition. The very fact that having in the proem emphasized to the exclusion of everything else the fabulous adventures, he immediately devoted the opening four books to an entirely different matter, the wanderings of Telemachus, is an indication that he was deliberately calling the attention of his audience to a part of the poem which, given its subject matter and relative brevity, might otherwise be dismissed as a thematic intrusion.

Why, then, did Homer not simply extend the matter of Books 9–12 and so allow them to bear structurally their own thematic weight? The answer is simple enough, given the scheme of the whole poem. Books 9–12, according to the proem, present a crucial period of development in the career of Odysseus. It must thus be prepared for (1) by defining the critical situation with which the hero eventually must deal, that is, the cleansing of his own palace (Books 1–4), and (2) by introducing him properly to the reader just before he comes to grips with that situation (Books 5–8). The major part of the book, in turn, must be given over to a detailed solution of that central problem, namely, to Odysseus's adventures on Ithaca. Such a plan and chronology meant that there was only one way in which the past adventures of Odysseus could be dealt with—by retrospective narrative—and Homer apparently invented the means, the beginning *in medias res,* to fit the need.[4]

The importance of the discovery that a story need not be told in strict chronological sequence cannot be overestimated nor its discoverer overpraised. The device of first establishing a situation and only then introducing one's hero into it has become the stock in trade of every television and motion picture writer; we are so used to learning for ourselves all the details of the corruption of the small western town before the new marshal arrives that we no longer even bother to analyze the technique. And flashbacks have all too often become the *dei ex machina* of the modern play, an easy way of handling a burdensome problem of exposition. But Homer may well have been the first author to attempt such techniques, and the very fact that he had to develop them shows clearly enough the difficulties of the structural problem he faced.

Books 9–12 presented yet another problem to Homer; in them the hero speaks for himself, and his account is thus a personal narrative, the record of his adventures as he sees them. Generally speaking, Homer is objective in his presentation of events: events and characters must speak everywhere for themselves; their author will not interpret them directly. Yet speak for themselves they do. By means of the poet's selection and emphasis patterns of meaning constantly emerge from the apparently objective text. In Odysseus's account of his own wanderings, however, the narrative point of view is limited even more stringently than usual. It would be singularly unconvincing for Homer to allow Odysseus to comment on the meaning of his own experience. The hero is too close to his adventures, for one thing; more important, we must see for ourselves in his actions the fruits of his wanderings if those experiences are to mean anything, dramatically speaking, to the poem. Thus, to pursue the point a bit further, Homer begins the poem by making clear what Odysseus himself cannot, that the early experiences of the hero are indeed meaningful in his development and hence are an integral part of the whole.

"He saw the cities of many peoples and he learnt their ways." The *Odyssey* begins and ends with cities, with the destruction of one, Troy, and the reestablishment of another, Ithaca. These two cities define the polar axis about which the poem revolves, as well as marking the beginning and end of the hero's journey. One city is destroyed by a woman, the other preserved by a woman. One is defeated by its licensing of passion, the other saved by its practice of decency. Between the two, Odysseus journeys, the sacker of one, the savior of the other.

Just inside this framework lie two more cities, Ismarus and Phaeacia, the first stop outward-bound and the last stop before home. And again the pattern repeats itself. To the first, Odysseus is a scourge, a destroyer, and a ravisher; in the second he is a guest and a friend of the court. In between stretch the wanderings. And although Homer was too skillful a writer to rely on an artificial and mechanical pattern of development, there are both progression and climax in these adventures.

After his escape from the cave of Polyphemus, the first fully narrated, though actually the third, adventure, Odysseus in his triumph and rage cannot resist revealing his identity to the blinded Polyphemus: "Cyclops, if anyone ever asks you how you came by your unsightly blindness, tell him your eye was put out by Odysseus, Sacker of Cities, the son of Laertes, who lives in Ithaca" (p. 153). One cannot conceive of a more complete calling card or a more prideful, more heroic gesture. The wounded giant standing on the cliff hurling great stones at the tiny boat below, the terrified crew protesting Odysseus's boasts "in gentle remonstrance," and the angry hero defying the giant and his father, the god Poseidon, with insult and abuse—it is a tableau more suited to the *Iliad* than to the *Odyssey* and a role more proper to Achilles than to Odysseus.

Yet at the beginning of his travels Odysseus obviously thinks of himself as another Achilles, a "Sacker of Cities." He destroys Ismarus, apparently without cause, killing its defenders, plundering its treasure, and kidnapping its women. No matter how much he blames his comrades for staying on or Zeus for sending the storm that follows, the attack upon the town is his responsibility, and it foreshadows the dis-

36

asters that follow. The whole episode is, in fact, a miniature Troy; though, according to the *Odyssey* if not to the tradition, Odysseus escapes the wrath of Athene upon those Achaeans who invaded her temple during the sack of Troy, he here incurs the wrath of Zeus by his brutal and unprovoked assault upon Ismarus.

Moreover, he comes off no better with the Lotus Eaters. For although he succeeds in saving his men from the enchantment of the natives, he does so by force rather than by any sort of intelligence, dragging them under the ship's benches and chaining them there.

With the Cyclops he endangers the lives of his comrades by deliberately seeking the cave of Polyphemus simply out of idle curiosity. Once captured, he uses his wits to escape, but again the blinding of the monster is an act of sheerest brutality and, as we have seen, his boasts from the ship are both vindictive and hubristic.

For the disastrous loss of the winds given him by Aeolus, Odysseus blames both himself and his sailors: "We came to grief," he says, "through our own criminal folly." Certainly the crew is principally to blame for having opened the bag of winds, but Odysseus's insistence on handling the sails alone and his not taking the crew into his confidence concerning the contents of the bag are instances of the continuing prideful behavior he had exhibited in taunting Polyphemus. Whatever the cause of their misfortune, the curse of Poseidon now governs the mariners' fate at sea, and Aeolus refuses to replace the lost winds on the grounds that "the world holds no greater sinner" than Odysseus (pp. 155, 157).

Odysseus's conduct in the encounter with the Laestrygonians is puzzling. As we have said, he practices what turns out to be a laudable precaution in anchoring his own ship outside the fateful cove. He makes, however, no attempt whatsoever to save the eleven ships inside the cove once the Laestrygonians attack, nor does he return once he has safely escaped. If he is not to blame for the destruction of his ships and men, he certainly cannot be credited with any attempt to rescue them.

37

Again on Circe's island, as in the encounter with Polyphemus, he sends his men, despite their protestations, to investigate the wisp of smoke he sees in the forest. This time, however, he goes alone to rescue those comrades who have been enchanted and is assisted by Hermes, who provides him with a drug for countering the witch's charms. Finally, though, he must rely on a threat of violence to force Circe to relent and restore his comrades to human form, although he goes to bed with her before attempting their transformation.

There are indications, moreover, that Odysseus might never have left Circe's realm had not his men pleaded with him and so touched his "proud heart." Interestingly enough, he tells Circe that he wishes to leave simply because his men "wear [him] out and pester [him] with their complaints" (p. 168).

His reaction to Circe's prophecy that he can never get home without first visiting Teiresias in the halls of Hades is noteworthy:

> This news broke my heart. I sat down on the bed and wept.
> I had no further use for life, no wish to see the sunshine
> any more. (p. 168)

This emotional reaction is very like that with which he has greeted all his previous misfortunes. The statement repeated each time he and his men left the scene of their disasters, that their joy at escape was "tempered by grief for the dear friends [they] had lost" (p. 154), is probably formulaic, but Odysseus himself in these early adventures seems more than conventionally prone to alternating fits of despondency and optimism. He feels apprehension and foreboding just before the encounters with Polyphemus and Circe. He almost commits suicide upon discovering that his men have lost Aeolus's friendly winds. He considers attacking Polyphemus alone, dons his armor to ward off Scylla singlehanded, and insists on dealing with Circe alone. Like his boast to Polyphemus, these actions are surely not those of a hero we have come to regard in the *Iliad* as a model of nimble-witted intelligence.

The role of Eurylochus is important in this regard. Howard Clarke calls him "nervous,"[5] and he is, but he also functions three times as a foil to Odysseus—once in refusing to lead Odysseus to Circe's house, again in urging the crew to refrain from following "this dare-devil Odysseus" (p. 167), and finally in urging Odysseus to allow the crew to land on Hyperion's island. It is Eurylochus also who persuades the crew to slaughter the cattle of the sun. He is, needless to say, not Odysseus's favorite (that role falls to Polites), and once Odysseus has to be refrained from chopping off Eurylochus's head.

The chief importance of Eurylochus, however, lies not so much in his own actions (he is simply a spokesman for the more recalcitrant members of the crew) but in the answers that his taunts provoke from Odysseus. To Eurylochus's suggestion after the capture of the twenty-two-man patrol that they all leave Circe's island immediately, Odysseus proudly replies that he will go alone to Circe's house. At Eurylochus's even more violent objection after the enchantment has been broken, that they all refrain from visiting Circe, Odysseus is restrained from violence only by a "chorus of remonstrance" from his men (p. 167). On the third occasion when Eurylochus rebukes his leader "in a truculent vein" (p. 196), Odysseus's answer is of a different quality entirely and marks, I believe, the beginning of a transformation in his attitude and personality.

This change in Odysseus's essential character is the result of his visit to the realm of Hades, and it was to demonstrate this shift in attitude, I am sure, that Homer so emphasized in the proem the wanderings of Odysseus, the fact that he learned from his travels, and his efforts on Hyperion's island to save his comrades. Certainly in his early travels he is prideful, occasionally cruel, emotionally unstable, and more often than not willing to sacrifice his men to satisfy his curiosity or to preserve his life. In short, he is the very model of an Achaean hero, a miniature Achilles who, lacking Achilles' overpowering prowess and grim integrity, alternately swaggers and weeps his way from catastrophe to catastrophe; he is, to be sure, the victim of Poseidon's wrath but the victim also of his own vanity.

But in the last of the fabulous encounters he seems changed. True, he ignores Circe's advice and tries to fight Scylla singlehanded, but it is to save the six men doomed to die that he does so. In approaching the Sirens he takes his men into his confidence for the first time, as he had not done when he kept secret the contents of Aeolus's bag of winds:

> My friends, [he says,] it is not right that only one or two of us should know the prophecies that Circe, in her divine wisdom, has made to me, and I am going to pass them on to you, so that we may all be forewarned, whether we die or escape the worst and save our lives. (p. 193)

And again, just before Scylla and Charybdis, he says:

> My friends, . . . we are men who have met trouble before. And I cannot see that we are faced here by anything worse than when the Cyclops used his brutal strength to imprison us in his cave. . . . So now I appeal to you all to do exactly as I say. (pp. 194–95)

But even more pointed is his response to Eurylochus's appeal on the grounds of fatigue and hunger that the crew be permitted to land on Hyperion's island:

> Eurylochus, I am one against many, and you force my hand. Very well. But I call on every man of you to give me his solemn promise that if we come across a herd of cattle or some great flock of sheep, he will not kill a head of either in a wanton fit of folly. (p. 197)

Moreover, in describing Odysseus's grief over the six men lost to Scylla, Homer abandons the formula he has hitherto used, in order to express more personally and more fully Odysseus's genuine anguish: "In all I have gone through as I made my way across the seas," he says, "I have never had to witness a more pitiable sight than that" (p. 196).

The interview with the dead is the beginning of this transformation, and it is for Odysseus not only a shattering experience but also a revelation. We do not know exactly why he goes to visit the dead except that Circe tells him he must, ostensibly to consult Teiresias. Yet Teiresias offers less helpful advice than does Circe later, and most of the prophet's speech concerns matters never touched upon in the *Odyssey*.

Let us examine in some detail Odysseus's experience outside the hall of Hades. Odysseus is prepared by Circe for what he is to see there; she tells him

> to consult the soul of Teiresias, the blinded Theban prophet, whose understanding even death has not impaired. For dead though he is, Persephone has left to him, and him alone, a mind to reason with. The rest are mere shadows flitting to and fro. (p. 168)

What Odysseus is to see, then, first of all is death itself, and though he is prepared by Circe, the horror of what he sees unnerves him:

> And now the souls of the dead who had gone below came swarming up from Erebus—fresh brides, unmarried youths, old men with life's long suffering behind them, tender young girls still nursing this first anguish in their hearts, and a great throng of warriors killed in battle, their spear-wounds gaping yet and all their armor stained with blood. From this multitude of souls, as they fluttered to and fro by the trench, there came a moaning that was horrible to hear. Panic drained the blood from my cheeks. (p. 172)

It is important that the first of the souls whom he greets is Elpenor, never "very much of a fighting man nor very strong in the head" (p. 170), the least, probably, of Odysseus's fallen comrades. In describing his most unheroic death in Book 10, Odysseus had uttered not a word of grief or regret, nor could he be bothered in his haste to bury him; yet here suddenly is Elpenor accusing Odysseus of neglecting his duty to a fallen comrade. In response to Elpenor's appeal

Odysseus makes a solemn promise to return to Circe's island and bury the body. And what is more, he does so, disregarding the inconvenience and delay it causes him. The end of the interview is touching—the two men, no longer prideful commander and foolish sailor, but simply living and dead, facing each other "in solemn colloquy" (p. 173).

Next approaches Anticleia, Odysseus's mother, who had still been alive when he left Ithaca. The hero's heart is moved by the sight of her; his "eyes filled with tears when [he] saw her there, and [he] was stirred to compassion" (p. 173). Yet true to Circe's warning, he will not allow her to approach the blood-filled trench. Teiresias must come first.

Teiresias begins his speech by warning Odysseus of the peril that awaits him on Hyperion's island. Yet that catastrophe is here presented to him only as a contingency, what may happen rather than what will happen. In this regard it is important to note that later Odysseus does in fact take every possible precaution against his crew's misconduct: he lands on the fated isle only after Eurylochus's accusation that he is deliberately playing the tyrant over his men and after warning the crew of the threat which hovers over them. Odysseus's failure to avert the disaster that follows the slaughtering of the sun god's cattle is thus in no way his fault; as the proem insists, "he failed to save those comrades, in spite of all his efforts."

Having repeated the curse of Polyphemus, the monster's prayer that Odysseus will return home "late, in evil plight, upon a foreign ship, with all [his] comrades dead" (p. 174), Teiresias goes on to inform Odysseus of the situation in Ithaca. This is presumably the hero's first knowledge of Penelope's difficulties, a matter on which Anticleia will comment briefly later. But Teiresias's fullest statement, strangely enough, is devoted to Odysseus's future after he has killed the suitors, the point at which the *Odyssey* ends. Odysseus, we learn, having cleansed his house, is to set out once more on his travels, on land and carrying an oar. He is to journey until he finds a people who know "nothing of the sea" and who mistake his oar for a winnowing-fan. There he will finally appease the wrath of Poseidon, and though his death will come gently "out of the sea," it will be after a long and prosperous reign (p. 174).

Most commentators on this passage, I think, follow the ideas of Dante (who probably invented the later wanderings of Odysseus) and of Tennyson; they regard Teiresias's prophecy as an indication that Odysseus will be, as Tennyson says, forever "roaming with a hungry heart," that he will wish always to "push off, and sitting well in order smite / The sounding furrows,"[6] leaving the governance of his island to the land-bound Telemachus. Yet such is clearly not the case; the whole point of the prophecy is that Odysseus will find peace only after he has abandoned the sea completely and has given, in a landlocked spot, a sign to Poseidon that his seafaring days are over. Death, moreover, will come to him not "at" sea but "out of" it, and indeed most accounts have him die on the Ithacan seashore at the hands of his son by Circe, Telegonus, who is leading an attack from the sea on what he mistakenly takes to be Corcyra.

The whole point of Teiresias's statement is thus that once home, Odysseus will cease to wander and will end his days after "an easy old age and surrounded by a prosperous people." In short, he will cease to be a "Sacker of Cities" and will become a king of Ithaca.

Odysseus's conversation with Anticleia reinforces this point, though with a different emphasis. His interest in Ithaca having been aroused by Teiresias, he answers her questions quickly and in no detail in order to get to what really interests him, the situation at home. About the troubles of Penelope and Telemachus, Anticleia is properly reticent and even evasive, obviously not wishing to worry Odysseus, but she says enough to make him uneasy, especially in the light of what he has already learned from Teiresias. She proceeds to talk at some length of what really interests her, the plight of Laertes wasting away in rags on a poor farm neglected by his son. And in the end she cannot resist blaming her son, however indirectly, for her own death.

It is, of course, a thoroughly motherly discourse, at once

a pardon and a rebuke. But it obviously touches a sensitive spot in Odysseus, as had Elpenor's plea. He has indeed been away too long sacking cities; his absence has resulted in turmoil in the state and in the life of his family; and he had better be getting home immediately to take upon himself the responsibilities of husband, father, and king.

There follows a long procession from the past, first a series of women, then of men. The women have one thing in common: all have suffered for love. All in one way or another thus suggest either Anticleia or Penelope and so remind Odysseus of his neglected duties at home. The men, however, are his old comrades in arms—Agamemnon, Achilles, and Aias. Agamemnon, of course, tells the story of his own fateful homecoming, but the heart of his remarks is his comments on Penelope and on Odysseus's own proper behavior upon returning home. Not that Odysseus has anything to fear from Penelope, Agamemnon insists; "Icarius' daughter is far too sound in heart and brain" to murder her husband. But, he adds, "women . . . are no longer to be trusted," and so Odysseus should not "sail openly into port" but should make a "secret approach" (p. 183).

Here, in the advice of Agamemnon, lies at least one of the keys to Odysseus's change of heart and later conduct. Both Teiresias and Anticleia have intimated that domestic trouble awaits him at home; neither has fully explained the extent of the trouble nor, more importantly, Penelope's relation to the suitors. Teiresias has said only that the suitors are "making love" to her, and Anticleia that she "has schooled her heart to patience." Agamemnon's remarks serve to undermine Odysseus's confidence still further, and it is important to the hero's development that he does in fact take seriously his former commander's advice: it is with the landing on Ithaca that we first observe fully the crafty, evasive Odysseus of the tradition. Only after he is at last on home ground and in the presence of unknown dangers do the lies and subterfuges begin and cunning displaces heroics as Odysseus's habitual course of action.

Achilles next approaches, and his demeanor and speech

44

are a shock to those who have known him in the *Iliad*. To Odysseus's compliment that he now reigns as a "mighty prince among the dead," Achilles replies:

> Put me on earth again, and I would rather be a serf in the house of some landless man, with little enough for himself to live on, than king of all these dead men that have done with life. (p. 184)

One can only remember here his great boast to Xanthus:

> Xanthus, you waste your breath by prophesying my destruction. I know well enough that I am doomed to perish here, far from my dear father and mother. Nevertheless, I am not going to stop till I have given the Trojans their bellyful of war.[7]

In the end the godlike wrath has become despair, and Achilles' words suggest that he now believes he chose wrongly, that it would indeed have been better for him to have preferred a long, obscure life, or any life at all, to his brief moment of glory before the walls of Troy.

Achilles, moreover, echoes a theme already introduced by Agamemnon. Both ask principally for some word of their sons and hence suggest to Odysseus that he might well consider the plight of his own son, Telemachus. He has been told by Anticleia that the boy is well and respected, but he must know from Teiresias's statement that Telemachus cannot control his mother's suitors and needs him at home.

The last shade to whom Odysseus speaks is Aias; the dead hero stands aloof, still pridefully harboring his grudge against Odysseus, who had defeated him in the contest for the arms of Achilles. Odysseus is diplomacy itself, blaming the gods for Aias's defeat, praising Aias's great strength, and begging him to curb his pride. "But Aias gave [him] not a word in answer and went off into Erebus to join the souls of the other dead."

In a famous description of this meeting W. B. Stanford says: "This is a scene unsurpassed in its sombre pathos— Roman rather than Greek in its majestic austerity. For a moment Ajax wins our admiration like a Cato or a Regulus. For a moment the flexibility of a Ulysses seems cheap and shoddy in the presence of this obdurate heroism. It is the last gesture in Homer of the older heroic style against the newer and more facile fashion."[8] Yet the scene taken in context may suggest just the opposite. How foolish of Aias to carry even into death his anger toward Odysseus! Here among the senseless, gibbering dead, the pride of Aias seems pointless, even pathetic. What good did the armor do Odysseus, or what good would it have done Aias? Was the momentary pique at losing a set of arms worth dying for? To Achilles, no; to Aias, yes: even in death he affirms by his stubborn silence the fact that he will always believe he was cheated and that his suicide was justifiable. Odysseus may indeed seem "cheap and shoddy" here; he is certainly not heroic. But he is alive and by now well on his way to a kingship and to a set of values which does not regard suicide as heroic but as irresponsible.

But death may be more than oblivion, and Odysseus last of all views the punishment of those who had sinned in life— Orion, Tityos, Tantalus, Sisyphus, and finally the greatest of all the mythical heroes, the mighty Hercules:

> Terrible . . . was the golden strap he wore as a baldric over his breast, depicting with grim artistry the forms of bears, wild boars, and glaring lions, with scenes of conflict and of battle, of bloodshed and the massacre of men. (p. 187)

The vision of the dead thus ends with those who have passed through heroism to cruelty and if, as Howard W. Clarke says, it presages the fate of the suitors,[9] it also must suggest to Odysseus the possible fate of an irresponsible sea captain.

When Odysseus returns to Circe's island to bury Elpenor, the change in him is beginning to be evident. He is now intent on reaching Ithaca; his new-found regard for his crew is manifest in his treatment of them; and by the time he reaches Phaeacia he is the considerate and diplomatic, yet also purposive and cunning, wanderer who will very shortly destroy his wife's suitors and reestablish his authority. From his interviews with the dead have come an awareness of the troubles that plague his home and a new conception of the responsibilities that await him there as husband, father, and king; an awakening to the horrors of death and the value of life; and a disillusionment with heroics and the heroic way of life.

Then why Odysseus's seven-year delay with Calypso? For one thing, the incident and presumably the length of time involved were parts of the received legend. It may be, as Clarke suggests, that the episode still retains some vestiges of a solar myth, that the "sojourn with Calypso occurs directly after the sin against the sun god" and so reflects "the period in the progress of the year-spirit when he is hidden, his powers enfeebled, waiting only for his time of return."[10] But this is not Homer's explanation. Athene makes it clear in the council of the gods that opens the *Odyssey* that Odysseus is a prisoner. Alone, without ships or men, he cannot leave Calypso. Nor would Poseidon allow him to escape had he means. It is in fact only the absence of Poseidon that permits the other gods to send Hermes to order his release.

Our first sight of Odysseus in captivity is instructive. Hermes could not find him in Calypso's cave, "for he was sitting disconsolate on the shore in his accustomed place, tormenting himself with tears and sighs and heartache, and looking out across the barren sea with streaming eyes." It is his habitual pose, we learn, for "life with its sweetness was ebbing away in the tears he shed for his lost home." But when Calypso first introduces the subject of his leaving, Odysseus clearly exhibits the craft which so marks his later journeys; he immediately suspects a trap and so draws from her an oath that she harbors "no secret plans for [his] discomforture" (pp. 90, 92, 93). And he counters beautifully, and without offending her, the nymph's arguments for his continued stay.

One effect of the structure of the poem is particularly important: we first see Odysseus after his initial adventures and his visit with the dead and therefore after the changes in his character have been accomplished. We see him first as he

47

will appear in the Ithacan adventures, and then we witness through his own narrative the process by which this character evolved. Our initial impression is thus of the kingly Odysseus, the shrewd diplomat who, arriving unknown and unclothed in Phaeacia, manages in a few hours to become guest of honor at a royal banquet. Phaeacia is, of course, the third of the book's four cities to be "conquered" by Odysseus. The first two, Troy and Ismarus, he sacks; this one he takes by guile, charming its princess and queen, beating its young men at their own games, and capturing with tales of marvels a ship and treasure from its king.

As nearly all the critics have said, Phaeacia is "over-civilized"; the Phaeacians' "life has no promise, no potentialities, no dynamism."[11] The island is a paradise, a garden where the fruit "never fails nor runs short, winter and summer alike." The Phaeacians are a peaceful people who take delight in "the feast, the lyre, the dance, clean linen in plenty, a hot bath, and . . . beds" (pp. 115, 128). Their island thus presents a contrast to the turmoil of Ithaca, but more important, it shows us the new Odysseus in action, and it also shows him resisting the refined overtures of Nausicaa, the subtle temptation to settle without difficulty into the role of king in a country not his own.

Howard Clarke has broken down the wanderings of Odysseus into "three categories of peril":

> First, irresponsibility (Lotus Eaters, Sirens, and Phaeacians), those who try to make Odysseus forget Ithaca and Penelope, try to tempt him to stay with them and give up his ties to home and family and country. Second, sex (Circe and Calypso), women who boast their superiority to Penelope, who even offer Odysseus immortality if he will stay with them as a kind of captive lover. The third category is violence (Cicones, Lestrygonians, Cyclopes), sub-human creatures whose interest in Odysseus does not go beyond destroying him and his men.[12]

While Clarke quite rightly refuses to allegorize the adventures, there is nevertheless a valid point to be made concerning the relationship of Odysseus's experiences to his development. For the three great dangers that he confronts are also temptations; specifically, they are the temptations which confront the hero—the irresponsibility to his cause or his group that results, as in Achilles, from an exaggerated emphasis on honor and prowess; the violence, again as in Achilles, that accompanies *hubris;* and sex, or rather the unrestricted adolescent pleasure that accompanies the violent, irresponsible heroic state of mind. These are essentially the forces that Odysseus meets and with varying degrees of success either conquers or escapes. He thus arrives in Phaeacia with neither ships nor men but naked and cleansed and ready for his new life.

Significantly, it is during his stay with the Phaeacians that Athene first appears to help him. True, her efforts on his behalf are at this point slight: she awakens Nausicaa and sends her to the beach, in the form of the young girl guides Odysseus to Alcinous's palace, assembles the Phaeacians for the entertainment, and marks Odysseus's discus throw. Still these actions prefigure her greater help to him in Ithaca; more important, because she is the representative of wisdom her appearance at this point indicates Odysseus's new-found reliance on intelligence and wit as a means of solving his problems.

Although most of the details of Athene's relationship with Odysseus are irrelevant to our discussion, one phase of their partnership is worth mentioning. Once in Ithaca, Odysseus begins an extended campaign of revenge replete with lies, disguises, and elaborate tactics for retaking the palace and destroying the suitors. The first of his lies is addressed to Athene herself, who appears in the form of a young shepherd. Not realizing who she is or even that he is at last in Ithaca, Odysseus questions the goddess and, having learned that he is indeed home, tells her an involved, though comparatively short, lie in which he represents himself as a Cretan fleeing justice. Having listened to his yarn, the "bright-eyed goddess smiled at Odysseus' tale and caressed him with her hand":

"What a cunning knave it would take," she said, "to beat you at your tricks! Even a god would be hard put to it.

"And so my stubborn friend, Odysseus the arch-deceiver, with his craving for intrigue, does not propose even in his own country to drop his sharp practice and the lying tales that he loves from the bottom of his heart. But no more of this: we are both adepts in chicane. For in the world of men you have no rival as a statesman and orator, while I am pre-eminent among the gods for invention and resource." (pp. 209–10)

They are birds of a feather, these two, and now that Odysseus has given up the posturing irresponsibility of the first books, she will indeed sponsor and shelter him until he reestablishes his kingdom. She approves of the lies and stratagems—he is "so civilized, so intelligent, so self-possessed," she says (p. 211)—and this approval by the wisest of the gods does much to remove the impression that Odysseus's craftiness in the last twelve books is both immoral and somehow degrading.

A change in the nature of Odysseus's antagonists in the second half of the poem also serves to define this shift in character from hero to king. In the fabulous voyages Odysseus fights principally against the forces of nature, particularly the sea itself in the person of Poseidon. His opponents are either natural forces such as Scylla and Charybdis or the monstrous inhabitants of a nature untamed by the civilizing hand of man—the Laestrygonians or Polyphemus. These forces, however, as we have seen, represent at least to some extent the untamed, natural bent of the uncivilized (in that word's literal sense) hero—his inclination toward violence, sex, and irresponsibility. What Odysseus is contending against here are thus not only the forces of physical nature but also his own all too animal nature, those qualities which make him a sacker rather than a builder of cities.

In the second half of the poem he turns his attention to the destruction of the suitors, who have abused the laws of civilization and are threatening his kingdom. And here, having destroyed, or at least escaped, the bestial, albeit heroic, forces within himself, he turns to their destruction in society. Moreover, he has gained in his travels the means of their destruction—intelligence. Violence, of course, he must use, but violence alone would never have freed Ithaca. The lies and stratagems, the councils of Athene, are the weapons of the politic and civilized man, and they are, at least in the *Odyssey*, the only ones that will work.

My contention that Odysseus goes through a transformation from hero to king links the *Odyssey* with the *Iliad*, where the two sets of values appear in two figures, Achilles and Agamemnon. And just as in the *Iliad* the origins of Achilles in myth and Agamemnon in history help Homer to support the thematic opposition for which these figures stand, so also in the *Odyssey* the ancestry of the figure of Odysseus supports his dual role in the poem.

W. B. Stanford speculates that the Homeric Odysseus may have descended from "two separate figures, one called something like *Odysseus*, the other something like *Ulixes*,"[13] the two figures having been joined together at some time before the writing of the *Odyssey*. There are unfortunately no traditional accounts, much less written records, of the identities or characteristics of these pre-Homeric figures. Yet it does not seem unreasonable to speculate, as does Robert Graves, that one of them, let us say the Odysseus figure, was a historical figure, a king of Ithaca who fought at Troy and for one reason or another was delayed in his homecoming.[14] The other, the Ulixes figure, may well have descended from myth, perhaps from a "pre-Greek sun-god . . . , or a solar divinity, or a year-daimon," as Stanford suggests;[15] or from a mythical king who obstinately "would not die when his term of sovereignty ended," as Graves says;[16] or from some form of the Indo-European Bear's Son's Tale, which has as its central theme "death in the midst of life, and some hope of life after the crushing calamity of death," as Rhys Carpenter thinks.[17] And perhaps joined to this myth is the tale familiar to all bodies of legend of a Wily Boy "whose cunning deceits delight their hearers and infuriate their victims,"[18] though this last I would not insist on.

A division between the adventures of the *Odyssey* traceable to each of the two pre-Homeric ancestors of Odysseus is at least hypothetically possible. Robert Graves states:

> The Odysseus legend would have included the raid on Ismarus; the tempest which drove him far to the southwest; the return by way of Sicily and Italy; the shipwreck on Drepane (Corfu); and his eventual vengeance on the suitors. All, or nearly all, the other incidents belong to the Ulysses story. Lotus-land, the cavern of the Cyclops, the harbour of Telepylus, Aeaea, Persephone's Grove, Siren Land, Ogygia, Scylla and Charybdis, the Depths of the Sea, even the Bay of Phorcys—all are different metaphors for the death which he evaded.[19]

It will be seen that such a division parallels almost exactly (the only difference lying in the assignments of four of the early adventures to the historical Odysseus) the division I have made, based on the poem itself, between Odysseus the hero and Odysseus the king. As in the *Iliad*, the hero derives from myth and the king from history. Exactly why this should be so in both poems I do not know; I doubt very much that Homer, however much he was aware of the contrast in values represented by hero and king, could have known much, or cared much, about their origins.

But certainly the mythical hero, whether sun god or Bear's Son, is an individualist who cares nothing for corporate values. He is ruled by his passions, for better or worse, and he is absolutely unyielding in the protection of his honor and integrity. It is part of the heroic code that Polyphemus should realize who has defeated him and so, disregarding his own welfare and that of his crew, Odysseus boasts to his victim of his victory.

I do not, however, wish to overstate the case. Some incidents in the early voyages of Odysseus are unheroic; W. B. Stanford cites, for example, his "ignominious escape from the Cyclops' cave."[20] But such examples are seldom found in Books 9–12. Those adventures which show Odysseus as the "much-enduring man"—his disguising himself as a beggar, his lying and deceitful conduct, his endurance of the suitors' humiliations—all come from the late sections, from a period in which Odysseus's self-discipline, sense of purpose, and determination to save the state have overcome his sense of personal honor.

As with the *Iliad,* however, one cannot say that Homer prefers the figure, or even the values, of king to hero. If the hero is on occasion whimsical or childish or emotional, the king is also on occasion "cheap and shoddy." We cannot really admire Odysseus's tactics, necessary though they are to his goal. He cannot, one realizes, act heroically under the circumstances, and he must subordinate heroic principle to kingly expediency. His virtues must be flexibility and accommodation, and if he loses his integrity and autonomy in the process, that loss is the price a king pays for a well-governed state and a happy household. He learns to govern his passions, to subdue his proud will, to forget his thirst for fame, and with the approval of the gods to accept his mission.

The so-called *Telemacheia,* Books 1–4, and the final passages of the poem are interesting in this regard since they present the opposite side of the coin, the case for heroic behavior, and so stand opposed to, or more properly in balance with, its Aristotelian middle. It is generally recognized that the *Telemacheia* is a kind of *Bildungsroman* recounting the maturing of Telemachus from a confused and ineffective adolescent to a purposeful and resourceful young man.[21] This change is accomplished by his exposure to the values of the heroic life; the domestic life of the palace he knows well enough already, and the only heroes he has met have been his mother's suitors, who are in every way degenerate and corrupt examples of the heroic type. Through Athene's prompting and guidance he visits Pylos and Sparta, Nestor and Menelaus, and there he receives what Clarke very properly calls an "initiation" and a "baptism" into the world of heroic values. He returns, successfully avoiding the ambush laid by the suitors, to assist his father in his great hour.

Moreover, the *Odyssey* ends, as it begins, with the search

of the son for the father, this time Odysseus for Laertes, and on the same note of initiation and transformation from domestic sterility to heroic accomplishment. Whatever the causes of Laertes' poverty and exile, he is in miserable straits indeed and needs, as had Telemachus, the revitalizing presence of Odysseus. Arising from the bath which follows his welcoming of his son, he is said to be "taller and sturdier than before" (p. 360), and with Athene's help he kills his man during the battle that follows.

Telemachus, like Laertes, must be awakened to the heroic virtues, and it is instructive that just before the battle Odysseus takes the occasion to remind Telemachus of the necessity for heroic conduct: "When you find yourself in the thick of battle, . . . I am sure you will know how not to shame your father's house," he says, and Laertes is delighted to see "[his] son and [his] grandson . . . competing in valour" (p. 364).

This reemphasis upon the heroic in the rejuvenation of Laertes may in fact help to explain a passage which has puzzled commentators and which is usually regarded as an intrusion upon the text—the descent of the suitors to the underworld. Most of the episode is given over to the suitors' rationalization of their own defeat, but what they say is enlightening. The scene begins with a conversation between Agamemnon and Achilles in which Agamemnon, thinking of his own ignoble fall, extravagantly praises the heroic manner in which Achilles died. "Yours was the happy death," he says, "with the flower of the Trojan and Achaean forces falling round you in the battle for your corpse." "Thus even death, Achilles," he concludes, "did not destroy your glory, and the whole world will honour you for ever" (pp. 352, 353).

Agamemnon's remarks contrast startlingly in tone and intent with Achilles' own observations in Book 11. We are, however, not allowed—deliberately, I believe—to hear Achilles' rejoinder, for Hermes appears at this point with the suitors. The long *apologia* of Amphimedon that follows is sheer rationalization, its central points being that the suitors acted as well-meaning gentlemen throughout their courtship and that they were assassinated by the evil and wily

54

Odysseus. Agamemnon, interestingly enough, ignores the main argument of Amphimedon's story and reacts only to that element in it which touches him personally, the faithfulness of Penelope as contrasted with the treachery of his own wife, Clytemnestra.

The *Telemacheia* and the last book of the *Odyssey* seem to me to balance the scales, to present the necessity and value of the heroic virtues. Telemachus must be awakened to action and Laertes from inactivity so that social order may be reestablished and the state preserved. And from one point of view, at least, Odysseus is everything the suitors maintain that he is—crafty, treacherous, and murderous.

The final word, however, comes from Athene and Zeus:

> Then Odysseus and his noble son fell on the front rank of the enemy and smote them with their sword and double-pointed spears. They would have destroyed them all and seen that none went home alive, if Athene, Daughter of aegis-wearing Zeus, had not raised a great cry and checked the whole of the contending forces: "Ithacans, stop this disastrous fight and separate at once before more blood is shed."
>
> Athene's cry struck panic into the Ithacans, who let their weapons go, in their terror at the goddess' voice. The arms fell to earth, and the men turned citywards, intent on their own salvation. The indomitable Odysseus raised a terrible war-cry, gathered himself together and pounced on them like a swooping eagle. But at this moment Zeus let fly a flaming bolt, which fell in front of the bright-eyed Daughter of that formidable Sire. Athene called out at once to Odysseus by his royal titles, commanding him to hold his hand and bring this civil strife to a finish, for fear of offending the ever-watchful Zeus.
>
> Odysseus obeyed her, with a happy heart. And presently Pallas Athene, Daughter of aegis-wearing Zeus, still using Mentor's form and voice for her disguise, established peace between the two contending forces. (pp. 364–65)

The poem thus ends, much as does the *Iliad*, in an ambivalent truce between its thematic opponents. Odysseus's natural inclination to heroics must again be checked by

Athene, in the form of the kindly, intelligent Mentor, who here calls him by his "royal," rather than his warlike, titles. Homer, looking back from a great distance, sees both old and new virtues, heroic and communal values, and like a god he holds them in a just balance. If in the end Achilles must yield to Agamemnon and the old Odysseus to the new, then history demands that this be so, but the glories of the heroic past remain in Homer to remind us of what has been lost.

CHAPTER THREE

Beowulf

Both the *Iliad* and the *Odyssey*, it will be observed, stand near the end of an oral tradition of literature. The extent to which the subject matter of this oral tradition preserved the actual history and usages of Mycenaean times cannot be definitely assessed; there was almost certainly a Trojan War involving a unified Achaean expeditionary force, and the description of certain pieces of equipment, notably Meriones' boar's-teeth helmet and Nestor's goblet, seem Mycenaean in origin. On the other hand, the Trojan War was almost certainly not fought over an abducted queen, and a number of details, the practice of cremation and the use of the chariot, for example, belong to Homer's own time. These confusions point to an amalgamation of past and present, not only of language and clothing and custom, but, more important, of historical fact and the legends and myths that had gradually become attached to it. Historical warriors become in this way the supermen of legend; and figures derived from gods, as well as the gods themselves, appear on the battlefield.

The oral tradition is also marked by an amalgamation of various linguistic forms and poetic techniques. Although the Ionic dialect was certainly basic in Homer's language, the so-called Aeolic veil which overlays that dialect, and the earlier Accadian-Cypriot forms which occasionally occur, helped to produce an artificial diction and language, itself a fusion of the archaic and the modern, "which made it possible for the singers in the oral tradition to choose forms in accordance with their immediate need."[1] Furthermore, gradually accumulated poetic devices such as the traditional lists and genealogies, the hexameter verse form, and the stock epithet governed and shaped whatever innovations and embellishments a poet might introduce.

Thus Homer, looking back along the continuum of history and literary tradition, had at his disposal a preformed matter and style which he could adapt to his own purposes and point of view. The lapse in time between event and poem allowed the past to impinge upon the present and the present to comment upon the past, the real to give credibility and solidity to the fictional and the fictional to give shape and meaning to the real. The poet had before him a vehicle that already contained to a large extent what the New Critics like to call irony, a balance between an attitude and its own contrary—in this case between the heroic and the antiheroic.

Note that it is a balance, not a rebuttal, and hardly even a contradiction. Homer saw life as steadily and as wholly as it is possible to do; he envisioned simultaneously and in perspective a former age as it actually was, as it was shaped over the years by the imagination of bards, and as it appeared to his own age. Free from both adulation and censure, he arrived at a vision of life and history seen, as far as man can ever see it, *sub specie aeternitatis*.

Important as they are in themselves, the so-called epic characteristics—the nationalistic hero, the vast setting, the superhuman deeds, the intervention of the gods—are best seen as arising out of the fusion of past and present values which lies at the heart of the Homeric poems. They, like the so-called epic devices—the opening statement of theme, the invocation to the Muse, the beginning *in medias res*, the descent into hell, the descriptions of arms, the lists and epithets—are finally, I think, simply means rather than ends. They are not themes but the forms and techniques which express themes.

Using these characteristics and devices to shape the received tradition, Homer gives it meaning and relevance. The *Iliad* and the *Odyssey* are in every sense moral poems, though they are never didactic; the poet's objectivity insures that no overt and clumsy preaching obscures either the action or the tone. Nevertheless, we are forced by the poet's selectivity and emphasis not only to observe but also to judge the action: we cannot remain neutral and unmoved at Achilles' killing of Lycaon or at Odysseus's meeting with Aias. These are moral actions in a moral world, not merely isolated vignettes of the far past.

The *Iliad* and the *Odyssey* are both principally concerned with man's relation to the state and therefore with a contrast of the values of the ancient, semilegendary heroic life and those of the new corporate society. But this theme is wide enough to encompass other themes as well: the essential moral stability of a universe in which Troy falls and kingly Odysseus reaches Ithaca despite the whimsicalities of Aphrodite and Poseidon, the efficacy of intelligence and reason as weapons against the ravages of violence and passion, the necessity for fidelity and justice in every age. And this thematic range and universality are possible in the Homeric epic only because the poet stands at the very end of the tradition which he shapes. As Jan de Vries observes, "one more step forward, and man takes the place of the hero."[2] It is indeed only a short step, in time as in space, from Homeric Ionia to Periclean Athens, and just as the king had replaced the hero, so in time the citizen replaced the king and with the king the bard and his heroic song.

From the evidence of the *Iliad* and the *Odyssey*, then, at least four historical factors combined to create the kind of heroic poetry that Homer wrote, though the existence of these conditions did not in itself guarantee the composition of such poetry: (1) an age distantly removed in the past from the poet and judged by his society to be in some sense heroic; (2) an oral tradition of the deeds of that faraway period, in which history, legend, and myth fused to form a literary image of it; (3) a new society, that of the poet, considerably more organized and stratified than that of the heroic age; and (4) the poet himself, standing at the very end of the oral tradition, capable of seeing past and present in relation to each other and of organizing traditional literary elements into a work which interpreted and judged the heroic age for his own time.

Such conditions need not be restricted to ancient Greece. Nor need the heroic age reflected in literature be heroic in our terms as long as it is so regarded in the eyes of the poet's society. Actually the late Mycenaean world which Homer celebrates seems in the light of modern historical findings to be more piratical than heroic and the prototypes of Agamemnon and Odysseus to be ruthless freebooters rather than great heroes.

The northern world of the early sixth century, the era of the great tribal migrations of the Scandinavian peoples, was likewise a period of violence. With the breakup of the Roman Empire restless invaders established small states throughout the North, and though it was a period of considerable wealth, it was also one in which Scandinavia, like the rest of Europe, was wracked by constant warfare between the new states. Judging from the chronicles, eddas, sagas, and genealogies that together form a loosely jointed, though generally coherent, picture of the times, Germania was plagued by unremitting tribal and intertribal warfare, by blood feuds, vendettas, and disputes over rightful succession, and by broken treaties and traitorous attacks. The general impression given by the early historians, say Jordanes or Saint Gregory of Tours, is of a restless and barbarous age, unredeemed by any standards of honor, generosity, or fair play, much less chivalry.

Yet the *Beowulf*-poet, looking backward from a vantage point some time in the first half of the eighth century, some two hundred years later, apparently sees in the events of those days the actions of a heroic society. Nor was he the creator of such an attitude. For whatever the actual facts of Germanic political and military life during these early centuries, the aristocracy of the many small kingdoms of Germania (which included Scandinavia and, from the late fifth century onward, England) thought of themselves as governed by a heroic standard of manners and actions. This was the so-called *comitatus* code first described by Tacitus at the end of the first century A.D. and still clearly adhered to at the battle of Maldon some nine hundred years later:

> The most powerful bond in this new society [that brought to England by the Saxons], whose being depended upon the security which had to be won and maintained by its own strength, . . . was that which united lord and man in a close relationship which was neither national nor tribal but personal. . . . Tacitus had been struck by the manner in which Germanic chieftains and their retainers were so closely united in bonds of loyalty that any who sought to win their own safety by withdrawing from battle after the death of their own chieftain would do so only at the cost of incurring lifelong reproach and infamy.[3]

Almost all Anglo-Saxon literature revolves about this personal loyalty of thane to leader. *Beowulf* itself records both the loyalty of Beowulf and Wiglaf to their kings and the dishonorable failure of Beowulf's thanes to support him in his fight with the firedrake. The *Wanderer* recounts the loneliness of exile from the *comites,* and the *Anglo-Saxon Chronicle* entry for 755 records the terrible dilemma of family versus tribal loyalty. The great battle poems of *Brunanburh* and *Maldon* graphically illustrate the way in which the *comitatus* code governed the actual military conduct of the period.

It would seem at first glance, therefore, that the conditions surrounding the composition of *Beowulf* do not even approximate those which resulted in the creation of the Homeric epics. Certainly the *Beowulf*-poet seems to have shared unquestioningly the ideals and values of the age and the society about which he is writing, values which can be shown historically to have been operative in Germanic Europe for nearly a thousand years. Whereas Homer wrote about a world considerably different from the one he lived in —a world in which governments of aristocrats had replaced those of kings, and commercial values the older heroic and individualistic ideals—the *Beowulf*-poet seems to have inhabited a court much like those of Hrothgar and Hygelac.

61

Yet a closer examination reveals that at least two major historical movements during the two hundred years separating Hygelac from the poet did result in changes in attitude; these changes, although they did not basically affect the broad scheme of values by which the Anglo-Saxon aristocracy lived, did in fact modify to some extent the personal relationship of thane and leader and are reflected in *Beowulf,* where they can be seen to underlie the conflicts and ultimately the meaning of the poem. The first of these movements is the bloody consolidation of the Northumbrian states in the sixth and seventh centuries[4] and the second the conversion of the island to Christianity.

According to most authorities, *Beowulf* is certainly of Anglian origin, although there has been some dispute over its exact date and place of composition. The linguistic evidence makes either Northumbrian or Mercian genesis possible, and Northumbria seems the logical choice because it afforded during the so-called Age of Bede "the necessary background for a highly cultured work of this kind."[5] The chief evidence for Mercian composition is the poet's mention of the fourth-century King Offa of the Angles, the ancestor of the Offa who ruled Mercia from 757 to 796. If this allusion is intended as a compliment to the Anglian ruler, then Mercian origin is certain, though a date during the reign of Offa seems somewhat late linguistically.

No matter from which of these great northern kingdoms the poem comes, the political situation in either must have been of some consequence to the poet. The early eighth century was in both kingdoms a comparatively peaceful respite from 150 years of constant struggle and unstable government: "For rather more than a hundred years after Caedwalla's abdication, although there were still some battles to be fought between the English kingdoms, there was a more settled order of society in which farmers were able to concern themselves with their lands, kings with the organisation of the means of government, and churchmen with the pursuit of spiritual life and the book learning which was its accompaniment."[6] But even though a temporary peace existed in which the arts might flourish, there were clear signs everywhere that the struggle for power in the North was far from over. Bede, who died in 735, foretells at the end of his history disturbances to come, and the rapidly shifting monarchy in Northumbria was itself an earnest of future bloodshed. The *Beowulf*-poet, whatever his place in society, wrote for an aristocratic audience; and he must have been keenly aware of the instability of his own as well as all other human societies, especially those based on the traditional *comitatus* code, on the "mere allegiance of individuals" in which the leader was forced, in order to maintain his position and the allegiance of his thanes, to expose himself to the greatest dangers and to take the greatest risks.

One would like to be able to produce some clear evidence of change in the governmental structure of Northumbria during the eighth century in order to contrast the poet's own age with that of his hero. Such evidence does not, of course, exist, though there are perhaps signs of an increasing awareness among the aristocracy of the need for a government based on some principle more stable than personal loyalty. The very fact of the immediate collapse of the empires of such powerful early kings as Edwin and Oswald shows how transient such states were, and the careers of Edwin and Penda demonstrate in what little regard these kings held any sort of firm and ordered governmental structure such as that imposed by European feudalism.

By the eighth century, however, at least some political changes were taking place, changes necessitated by the growth in territory and hence in complexity which accompanied the consolidation of the smaller kingdoms. After the conversion governmental functions became even more complex when the problems of church lands and remission of taxes arose. There is evidence that by the middle of the ninth century Wessex had been subdivided into shires, and it is more than possible that similar allocations of land and responsibility had occurred earlier in the northern kingdoms.

Certainly by the eighth century the concept of monarchy had changed somewhat from the early days of Anglo-Saxon rule. There is a strong possibility that the first kings were simply "adventurers whose prowess in war enabled them to maintain a band of warriors."[7] As time passed, the hereditary principle became strengthened, as is evidenced by the desire of the English royal families to demonstrate their lineage. And as the territorial possessions of the major kings increased and their governments became more complex, they necessarily became administrators as well as soldiers. By the time of Alfred "the monarchy stood at the apex of a variety of institutions which served the purposes and met the needs of local government with such efficiency that they continued to form the framework of administration for long after the Norman Conquest." Such an elaborate system was certainly not created within a few generations but "came gradually into being over several centuries,"[8] and it is possible to see in the reigns of Offa and Aldfrith the beginnings of an order of kingship based on administrative concern and ability rather than sheer physical prowess and personal loyalty.

The usual statements that the *comitatus* idea of personal loyalty dominated the lord-thane relationship might therefore be somewhat modified to include a semblance of national feeling from the eighth century onward, particularly in the concept of kingship. There is at least some contrast to be made between the small, exceedingly intimate court group depicted in *Beowulf* and the rather more complex and stratified aristocracy in which the poet must have actually lived. However strongly the court of Offa or Aldfrith may have paid allegiance to the *comitatus* code in its insistence on personal, rather than national, loyalties, its glorification of a warrior king dedicated only to personal honor was already becoming a memento of the past, a slogan rather than a guideline, a statement of principle rather than of operation.

Certainly *Beowulf* itself is concerned throughout with political warfare and its consequences. Beowulf's personal history is played out against a background of the rise and fall of the great Scandinavian powers, especially the Danes and the Geats. Allusions to events both preceding and following the dramatic date of the action constantly remind us of the tragic fate of tribes and rulers. After three generations of conquest and glory, Hrothgar's kingdom, already demoralized by the ravages of Grendel, is to be rent during the aged king's lifetime by the attack on Heorot by the Heathobards under Ingeld, and after Hrothgar's death by Hrothulf's seizure of the Danish throne. The Geatish raiders are conquered by the Swedes following the death of Hygelac, and though Beowulf is permitted to rule for fifty years in peace, the prophecies of Wiglaf leave little hope for the future of the Geatish nation. The poet alludes also to the famous Ostrogothic King Eormanric who lost his empire and his life to the Huns in the fourth century, to the internal struggles for power within the Swedish royal house, to Heremod's seizure of the Danish throne, and to the feud between Frisians and Danes which erupts into violence in Finn's hall—all instances of the inability of the Scandinavian nations to maintain anything resembling a stable and secure government for more than a few generations.

I would maintain that both in the traditions of the Germanic heroic age and in the events of the century preceding his own, the poet saw evidence of the failure of the heroic *comitatus* code, with its insistence on personal allegiance, to create and maintain peace and order and that his concern over, or at least his perception of, this failure dictates to a large extent both the structure and what we might call the political theme of the poem.

No one can, of course, determine exactly the form or content of the heroic lays that constituted the raw material of *Beowulf*. Most critics agree that while no single archetype for the poem ever existed, the poet did inherit a vast amount of legendary and verse tradition which he uses. His artistic problem was thus roughly analogous to that of Homer: selecting and shaping his received materials into some sort of ordered and meaningful poetic structure. The characters and events of the poem may therefore be traditional, but their relationships and meaning are, as in the *Iliad* and *Odyssey*, the poet's own.

While the structure of *Beowulf* is still much debated, no

one, I think, any longer holds seriously the opinion of older critics such as W. P. Ker that *Beowulf* is essentially unstructured. The great hiatus, the fifty-year caesura, which divides the poem is clearly an intentional structural device, and most critics would probably accept, with individual modifications, J. R. R. Tolkien's statement that the poem is a "contrasted description of two moments in a great life, rising and setting; an elaboration of the ancient and intensely moving contrast between youth and age, first achievement and final death."[9]

I think that Tolkien is accurate in his observation, but I think also that there are further contrasts to be developed, notably those between hero and king and between Christian and pagan. The Beowulf of the first part of the poem is in every way the ideal Germanic hero, the perfect thane. He comes to Hrothgar's court to repay, very properly, a family obligation (Hrothgar had paid the compensatory *wergild* on behalf of Ecgtheow, who had slain a Wylfing named Heatholaf) and also to gain glory, to establish a reputation for heroism after a misspent youth. The structure of the first half of the poem is so arranged as to stress Beowulf's heroism. As in the *Odyssey*, the tragic situation in Hrothgar's court is established first—at the same time, by the way, that the political theme is introduced by way of the rise and fall of the Danish nation—and only then is the hero introduced into the action. Beowulf is allowed, moreover, to present his credentials and purpose in proper heroic style three times: to the coast guard, to Wulfgar, and to Hrothgar. Unferth's challenge and Beowulf's account of his swimming match with Breca are introduced to demonstrate before the encounter with Grendel some proof of Beowulf's prowess and to allow him to make his great vaunt. He accepts proudly, yet also graciously, the rewards tendered him by Hrothgar and does not hesitate to undertake the pursuit of Grendel's dam. Once home among the Geats, he reports faithfully to Hygelac and turns over to his lord the Danish treasures. He is in every way the very model of a Germanic hero—loyal, brave, incredibly strong, and above all eager for praise.

Yet the heroic tone of the first section of the poem is undercut by foreshadowings and contradictions. By allusions we are made constantly aware not only of the shadow which overhangs the Danish court but also of future tragedies in Beowulf's own life. The burial of Scyld foreshadows the funeral of Beowulf; the burning of Heorot, the destruction of Beowulf's own hall; the swimming match with Breca, Beowulf's escape from the battle with the Frisians, in which Hygelac perishes; the impotency of Hrothgar's thanes, the failure of the aged Beowulf's companions; the allusions to Heremod and Hrothgar's "sermon," the effect of pride upon a good king; the grief of Hildeburgh, the sorrow of Hygd.

There are also important differences between the two encounters of the first part of the poem. Beowulf conquers Grendel with his bare hands, unaided by his retainers. In the fight with Grendel's mother, however, his life is saved by his armor, by the direct intervention of God, who allows him to break the monster's hold, and by a magical sword to which his attention is called, presumably by God. In short, in this second encounter mere heroism and natural strength can no longer insure victory as they did in the swimming match and in the fight with Grendel, and we are to see, I think, that Beowulf's triumph here is attributable more to God's grace than to his own efforts. In fact the first half of the poem, despite its heroic matter and tone, implies that mere heroism cannot always cope with the problems which threaten either a nation or an individual, and so the first half serves both to undercut the heroic ideal which forms its surface action and to prepare us for what is to come later. Hrothgar through age and Unferth through failure have come to doubt the magic of unaided heroism: Unferth's bitter, drunken attack on the reputation of the young hero and the tired, disillusioned Hrothgar's sermon on pride and age are indications that these men are perhaps more worldly wise than the cocky young stranger standing before them, to whom in time a similar wisdom may come. The covert appeal of Wealhtheow to Hrothulf, on the grounds of both *comitatus* and family loyalty, to protect the rights of her own sons is no more than an ineffective gesture. And the whole composite of allusions hovering just behind the façade of youthful, heroic triumph —allusions to proud Heremod and cursed Sigemund, to feuding Finn and Hengest, and to the other figures of history the facts of whose lives were known well enough to the poet's audience—all make a single point, that the insistence of the *comitatus* code upon personal loyalty leads inevitably to family feuds and vendettas and, because of the intimate and unavoidable connection between personal and national loyalty, to treachery and war.

The failure of the *comitatus* code, moreover, dominates the second half of the poem. As A. G. Brodeur points out, the tragic conflict between the two parts is strikingly clear: Hygelac is dead, the Danes have been destroyed, and Beowulf, now an old man, has ruled his fifty years like Hrothgar and is faced with Hrothgar's problem—a deadly monster and a group of cowardly thanes. Even before the dragon appears, the poet forecasts the death of Beowulf and begins to anticipate with increasing frequency the approaching destruction of the Geatish nation. And although Brodeur insists that the contrast between the closing lines of Part 1, which show "the hero at home in his uncle's court . . . , Hygelac . . . alive and powerful, his realm . . . rich and strong," and the beginning of Part 2, with its "terrible antithesis" to Part 1, is "sufficient in itself, without irony,"[10] the comparison between Hrothgar and the Beowulf of Part 2 is surely both intended and ironic. Suddenly the young hero who saved an old king is himself an old king, the slayer of dragons is about to be slain by a dragon, the savior of Heorot finds his own hall destroyed, and he who had ridiculed Hrothgar's untrustworthy thanes is now surrounded by cowards.

If we are to make sense of Beowulf's last foreboding, bitter speeches, and hence of the second half of the poem, we must read them in this context. For they are not the speeches of a successful Christian king who is satisfied with the fruits of his life's work and, having made his peace with God and secured the future welfare of his nation, is assured of his place in history and among the saints. Even his last apologia (ll. 2724–51) is filled with regret that he has no son, that

Fate has deprived him of kinsmen, that his only monument will be a hoard of treasure. He takes pride, of course, in the fact that he has kept the peace and has not sworn many unjust oaths or stooped to cunning attacks or killed his own kinsmen. But these are mainly negative accomplishments and are hardly the boasts of a triumphant and accomplished ruler. These final speeches make clear Beowulf's realization that his struggles have been for the most part in vain, that Wiglaf is the last of the Waegmundings, and that the Geats are doomed. In the end his only thanksgiving to God is for the treasure he has been able to win for his people, a treasure which, ironically, is buried with him.

The picture of Beowulf presented in these scenes, especially in Section 33, which immediately precedes the fight with the dragon, is disturbing in a number of ways. The poet says of him that he thought that by "breaking established law [*ealde riht*], he had bitterly angered God, the Lord everlasting. His breast was troubled within by dark thoughts, as was not his wont."[11] The usual interpretation of these lines is that suggested by Klaeber, that Beowulf "did not yet know the real cause of the dragon's ravages."[12] Both Klaeber and Wrenn take the *ealde riht* to which the poet refers to mean God's commandments, but the poet has made no mention of Beowulf's breaking any such laws, and it may well be that the passages of Section 33 following the statement of Beowulf's despair are actually attempts to explain the nature of the *ealde riht* that Beowulf has violated.

Having described the ravages of the firedrake and prophesied again the deaths of both Beowulf and the dragon, the poet tells us that Beowulf

> scorned to seek the far-flier with a troop of men, with a great host. He feared not the fight, nor did he account as aught the valour of the dragon, his power and prowess; because ere this, defying danger, he had come through many onslaughts, wild attacks, when he, the man of victory, purged Hrothgar's hall.[13]

This passage, coming immediately after one of the many prophecies of Beowulf's death, emphasizes the hero's self-confidence and great pride in his own strength, qualities which seemed perfectly fitting in the young hero but are strangely out of place in an old king brooding on his transgressions. The poet seems to be establishing here yet another comparison with Hrothgar and, incidentally, with Hygelac, this time in terms of their pride: Hygelac's raid against the Frisians so weakened the Geats that they were unable to aid Hrothgar's sons in their struggle with Hrothulf; Hrothgar in his pride had built Heorot, only to find that he could not inhabit it. Similarly, in his self-assurance that he is still the same man who fifty years earlier defeated Grendel and his mother, Beowulf here scorns the safety of numbers. Taken in this context, the sermon on humility delivered by Hrothgar to the young Beowulf suddenly makes sense, not as a pagan king's Christian exposition of the follies of pride but as an explicit warning to Beowulf of the trap into which any aged king may fall—regarding himself as immune to the ravages of old age and faltering judgment and therefore believing that he is still a youthful hero subject only to the laws of heroic behavior.

Moreover, the next few verses provide an alternative, or more likely a supplementary, explanation of Beowulf's depression, though one which is at first glance confusing. Recounting the death of Hygelac at the hands of the Frisians, the poet says that Beowulf alone escaped the battle by swimming, this time carrying thirty suits of armor, "over the stretch of the gulfs"[14] back to his homeland. Although this incident is another example of Beowulf's remarkable strength and skill in swimming, it is out of keeping with our idea of the Germanic hero and of the *comitatus* spirit, which demanded, above all, loyalty even unto death in battle. We should have expected Beowulf, the perfect hero, to have died at Hygelac's side, and it may well be that his flight is the violation of an *ealde riht* of the *comites* which he recalls and laments at the end of his life.

The next few lines (2369–79), however, explain the poet's purpose in introducing Beowulf's flight from the Frisians by emphasizing his failure in the past to understand

the laws of both kingship and *comites*. The poet recalls that
when Beowulf returned to the Geats, Queen Hygd, dis-
trusting her own son's ability to protect the kingdom, offered
Beowulf the crown and that he refused it, as Adrien Bonjour
says, "out of sheer loyalty towards the rightful heir"[15]—the
proper *comitatus* attitude. Subsequent events prove that it
would have been better for his countrymen if Beowulf had
accepted the queen's offer. Heardred is killed by the Swedes,
and the war between Swedes and Geats culminates in an uneasy truce which lasts only during Beowulf's lifetime. Although I agree with Bonjour that one purpose of the refusal
is to establish still another image of Beowulf's power, I think
that the poet, by placing the passage so close to the descriptions of the dragon's ravages and Beowulf's enduring pride,
and in conjunction with his retreat from Hygelac's battle with
the Frisians, quite definitely suggests a basic confusion in the
hero's attitude. He runs away from the Frisians in violation
of the heroic code. Presumably, since it is impossible to make
Beowulf out to be a coward, his action is dictated by a desire
to help safeguard the Geatish nation against the attacks
which will inevitably follow. Yet, once home, he refuses on
the basis of *comitatus* loyalty to take the step that would insure the welfare of his nation: to accept the throne.

An account of Beowulf's revenge upon Onela for the
death of Heardred follows immediately and quite naturally;
here again, the poet's aim may be to explain Beowulf's melancholy in terms of his having broken the *ealde riht* of both
kingship and *comites*. Beowulf, of course, supports Onela's
nephew in his revolt against Onela, an engagement that results in the uncle's death. Yet one must wonder at Beowulf's
action since the text clearly states that after Heardred's
death Onela departed for Sweden and permitted (*let*) Beowulf to hold the Geatish throne. I strongly suspect also that
the *god cyning* of line 2390, whose attitude toward Beowulf
is here praised, is Onela. If this reading is correct, then
Beowulf's later action against Onela is inexcusable; it is the
action of a proud Heremod who becomes improperly involved
in what we should call the internal affairs of another nation,

striking down a benefactor and overlord for the sake of revenge.

It is certainly possible that I am here guilty of over-reading, or perhaps even misreading, the text, that—as the commentators have maintained—the poet introduces these incidents not to bury Beowulf but to praise him. Yet the allusions to Beowulf's pride, his escape from the battle with the Frisians, his refusal of the Geatish crown, and his role in the death of Onela, coming as they do immediately after the description of his melancholy and his feeling that the dragon's onslaught is a result of his somehow breaking *ealde riht,* may perhaps serve to explain his dejection.

In short, far from extolling the heroic attitude, the poem taken as a whole decries it. As the poem progresses, Beowulf's actions against his opponents become more and more fool-hardy and hence less and less justifiable in terms of his people's welfare. Throughout, Beowulf follows "a code that exalts indomitable will and valour in the individual, but so-ciety requires a king who acts for the common good, not for his own glory."[16] Nevertheless, one cannot say that the poem wholeheartedly extols the ideal of kingship, or at least a kingship based on heroic ideals. King Hrothgar is certainly incapable of dealing with the problems that confront him, and even Beowulf after fifty years of prosperous rule has not established a nation that can survive him. As we have seen, his desertion of Hygelac is best explained by the hero's realization, however dim and intuitive, that it will be best for the nation for him to return home alive; yet he im-mediately returns to heroic standards in refusing Hygd's offer of the throne and later in attacking Onela. However, upon his accession to the throne he apparently rules the Geats in a peaceful and kingly, as distinct from an aggressive and heroic, fashion by maintaining stability rather than seeking to acquire lands and glory. We are told that he ruled for fifty years and that he was a "wise king, an old guardian of the land."[17] Later, near the point of death, he says to Wiglaf:

> I have ruled this people for fifty years. There was no people's king among the nations about who durst come

against me with swords, or oppress me with dread. I have lived the appointed span in my land, guarded well my portion, contrived no crafty attacks, nor sworn many oaths unjustly.[18]

Despite his efforts to maintain the peace, however, the dragon in the end seeks him out, as it had Hrothgar, and in his terror he assumes again the role of hero, attacking the dragon without help, only to find that he must now, like the aged Hrothgar, rely upon a young hero to save him.

It may well be, in fact, that the failures of both Beowulf and Hrothgar to deal adequately with their monstrous invaders reflect something of the pagan concept of sacral kingship. Beginning with Frazer, anthropologists and literary critics have seen as a ruling motif both in primitive society and in literature the ritual sacrifice of the sacral king as a means of assuring the continuing fertility of the land and prosperity of the tribe. In *The God of the Witches* Murray says:

> The underlying meaning of the sacrifices of the divine victim is that the spirit of God takes up its abode in a human being, usually the king, who thereby becomes the giver of fertility to all his kingdom. When the divine man begins to show signs of age he is put to death lest the spirit of God should also grow old and weaken like its human container. . . . When the changes inevitable to all human customs gradually took place, a substitute could suffer in the king's stead, dying at the time the king should have died and thus giving the king a further lease of life.[19]

One need not accept Murray's highly conjectural theories regarding Joan of Arc and Thomas à Becket as substitute victims to grant the basic truth of her assertion that the sacrifice either of the king or of his substitute was a fundamental part of the Germanic paganism which infused England in the Anglo-Saxon period and continued well into the Christian era. The *Ynglinga saga* records that the Swedish King Domaldi was sacrificed by his people to improve a series of bad harvests, and Snorri records that Olaf the

Woodcutter, one of the ancestors of the kings of Norway, was sacrificially burned in his house after a number of crop failures. And almost certainly the old sacrificial rituals, as E. K. Chambers says, lingered "in the country, the pagan, districts" and so "passed silently into the dim realm of folklore," most notably in England, in the village festival play.[20]

I would hardly claim that *Beowulf* is filled with references to human sacrifices, disguised for court consumption by a pagan poet posing as a Christian. But I think it entirely possible that the poem does reflect something of the pagan notion of kingship and ritual sacrifice. No one would deny that after fifty years as king, Hrothgar has outlived his period of effective rule. Old age has robbed him of his youthful strength. His dreams of glory in building Heorot have been shattered by the raids of Grendel, who in twelve years has completely demoralized the Danish court: the thanes no longer attempt to sleep in the hall at night, nor will Grendel consent to be bought off. Hrothgar himself is powerless even to approach his own throne, and in desperation the court abandons whatever shallow Christianity it had professed and turns to pagan gods. In Murray's terms the "spirit of God" has grown old within Hrothgar and has weakened "like its human container." Nor, apparently, can Hrothgar's son deal with the situation. The task of cleansing Heorot thus falls upon the young Beowulf, who replaces the old king in destroying Grendel and his mother and who is almost, but not quite, accepted by Hrothgar as foster son and heir.

His ineffectualness in dealing with Grendel is not the only sign of Hrothgar's decrepitude. Ingeld's revolt during the old king's lifetime and Hrothulf's seizure of the throne after his death are attributable to Hrothgar's senility and lack of judgment. Wealhtheow plainly shares the king's failing and clearly evidences it in her trust of Hrothulf and in her plea to Hrothgar to be generous first of all to his own kinsmen, leaving to them, not to Beowulf, his subjects and kingdom. It is noteworthy that after Wealhtheow's speech Hrothgar never again alludes to the "new kinship" he has offered Beowulf; instead he proposes rewards of gold and riches for the killing of Grendel's mother and, after Beowulf has successfully destroyed this second menace, sends him home to Hygelac with a sermon on humility and the prayerful hope that in time Beowulf will become king of the Geats and will remain friendly to the Danes.

The point is, I think, that Hrothgar is allowed to live too long; that his prolonged rule brings about the destruction of his nation; and that Beowulf, who might have assumed Hrothgar's throne by virtue of having saved the Danes, does not do so or, if he does, does so only after the forces of revolt have destroyed the nation.

The same point may be made about Beowulf in his old age. The Beowulf of the second half of the poem is not the hero of the first. Fate, youth, his thanes, and at the end even his boundless self-assurance have deserted him. It is Wiglaf who now comes to the fore and, like the young Beowulf, is seen by his lord as a foster son. Yet again the substitution comes too late, and the words of Wiglaf, whom the Swedes hate, and of the messenger leave us in no doubt of the heavy days to come. Having ruled too long, the old king dies, and with him the nation whose welfare had depended upon his strength and virility.

It may be objected that this is a strange line to take concerning a poem which has nearly always been taken as a paean of praise for the heroic attitude as exemplified by Beowulf. Yet the poem does not conclude in triumph but with the death of Beowulf and the forecast destruction of his nation, and these tragedies are unrelieved by even a hint that they have been in any way worthwhile, that either man or nation has accomplished anything of value by them. In the end, no matter how great the personal valor, how loyal the *comites*, how determined the heroic struggle, even how effective the reign, the dragons prevail and Heorot burns.

The much-discussed combination of Christian and pagan elements not only reinforces this interpretation but also adds to it a third concept of behavior, the Christian. One has only to glance at the criticism devoted to *Beowulf* in the last sixty years to see how firmly entrenched the so-called Christian interpretation of our chief Anglo-Saxon poem has become. Specialized studies, such as M. B. McNamee's in-

terpretation of the poem as an "allegory of salvation,"[21] Marie
Hamilton's view of it as reflecting the Augustinian doctrines
of grace and providence,[22] and the patristic studies of D. W.
Robertson, Jr., R. E. Kaske, and Morton W. Bloomfield,[23] as
well as the more general treatments of A. G. Brodeur and
Dorothy Whitelock,[24] have apparently solidified Klaeber's
original assertion: "Predominantly Christian are the general
tone of the poem and its ethical viewpoint."[25] Such studies
have thoroughly discredited the early arguments of H. M
Chadwick and F. A. Blackburn[26] that the Christian sentiments
expressed by both characters and poet are mere "colorings"
in a poem which "once existed as a whole without the
Christian allusions."[27] And certainly no student would wish
to argue against the more recent scholars that the *Beowulf*-
poet and his audience were not possessed of the rudiments of
Christianity or that, save perhaps in a few passages (ll. 168–
69, 180–88, 1740–60), the Christian sentiments expressed in
the poem as it has come down to us are not part of its original
design.

Yet one feels that here again the scholars may have pro-
tested too much. The subject matter, the narrative line and,
more important, the tone of *Beowulf* are far removed from
the patently Christian poems of the Old English period, not
only the saints' lives and biblical paraphrases but also those
poems that, like *Beowulf*, boast a strongly heroic character.
The difference between *Beowulf* and these poems is ultimately more qualitative than quantitative: it is not so much a
matter of more or less Christian "coloration," or even of more
or less specifically Christian subjects, as it is a matter of point
of view, language and diction, and especially of tone. Com-
pare for a moment the ending of *Beowulf* with the closing
passages of *Judith* and *Andreas*, which, although they derive
from the Old Testament and Christian folk tradition rather
than specifically Christian scriptural sources, nevertheless
share with *Beowulf* the heroic attitude:

> *Judith:* Judith ascribed the glory of all that to the Lord of
> hosts who endued her with honour, fame in the realm of
> the world and likewise reward in heaven, the meed of

victory in the splendour of the sky, because she ever held true faith in the Almighty. At the end she doubted not at all of the reward which long while she had yearned for. Therefore glory for ever be to the dear Lord who in his mercy created the wind and the airs, the skies and spacious realms, and likewise the fierce streams and the joys of heaven.[28]

Andreas: And then they worshipped the Lord of glory, called aloud all together, and spoke thus: "There is one eternal God of all creatures! His might and his power are famously honoured throughout the world, and his glory gleams over all on the saints in heavenly majesty, with beauty in heaven for ever and ever, eternally among the angels.[29]

Beowulf: The warriors began to rouse on the barrow the greatest of funeral fires; the wood-reek mounted up dark above the smoking glow, the crackling flame, mingled with the cry of weeping—the tumult of the winds ceased— until it had consumed the body, hot to the heart. Sad in heart, they lamented the sorrow of their souls, the slaying of their lord; likewise the women with bound tresses sang a dirge . . . the sky swallowed up the smoke.[30]

It should be obvious, even from these brief quotations, that while *Judith* and *Andreas,* like *The Fates of the Apostles* and *The Dream of the Rood*—all of which end with death and unhappy events—conclude with paeans of triumph and rejoicing in the victories of God's servants, *Beowulf,* save for a single reference to Beowulf's soul having sought the judgment of the righteous, ends in tragedy and disillusionment. As we have seen, Beowulf's death, however heroic it may have been, has unleashed the forces that will destroy his people, and the last three hundred lines of the poem, despite all the appeals of Whitelock to "things that last for ever,"[31] are pessimistic and foreboding in the extreme.

The difference between *Beowulf* and these other poems, moreover, lies not only in the fact that *Beowulf* ends tragically and the others victoriously, for the whole of *Beowulf,* despite its Christian and heroic elements, is strongly and most un-

Christianly and unheroically pessimistic in its view of life and history. The narrative framework of the poem, the story of Beowulf's encounters with his monstrous opponents, demonstrates that although even the most heroic of men may for a time overcome the powers of darkness, he will eventually be defeated by them. The background of Scandinavian history before which the action of *Beowulf* takes place and to which the poet constantly alludes makes precisely the same point about the fates of nations: societies rise only to perish, and it is only a few generations from Scyld Scefing to Hrothulf and from Hrethel to Wiglaf. It is thus no surprise that *Andreas,* which reflects an essentially optimistic, Christian philosophy of history, ends with the saint's followers praising the everlasting glory of God and his saints, while *Beowulf* concludes with a lonely funeral pyre and the lamentations of the Geats.

I bring forward this pronounced difference in tone between *Beowulf* and these patently Christian poems not to deny the presence of the many obviously Christian sentiments in *Beowulf* but simply to reassert in the face of almost all recent criticism the essential paganism of the poem. However important the principal Christian elements may be— the allusions to free will, Hrothgar's sermon on humility, Beowulf's moderation and thanksgivings to God, the identification of Grendel with the race of Cain—they are essential neither to its narrative nor even to its major theme: the unyielding, though profitless, struggle of man against the forces of a malevolent nature. In the final analysis the Christian elements are peripheral; they are not required in a paraphrase of the poem, they contribute nothing to its overall effect, and they in no way affect either its structure or its thematic unity.

More important, however, is the fact that in concentrating upon the Christian elements of the poem, critics have failed to plumb the depths of its paganism. For although its Christianity is at best conceived of as a surface design, its paganism is the very fabric of the poem. It is a comparatively easy process, for instance, to amass evidence to show that at the time the poem was written, the stern Germanic Wyrd (like Dame Fortune) had become softened and shaped into an agency of the Christian God; indeed, it may have been so considered by the poet. But the action of the poem, if not always the comments of characters and author, asserts man's fate to be fixed and tragic; as Charles Kennedy has remarked, there is no evidence either in plot or in tone "to imply control of Fate by the superior power of Christian divinity."[32]

Hrothgar's speech on humility may well be an interpolation, but even if it is not, its sentiments are hardly in agreement with what we know of Hrothgar's actions in the poem; Brodeur, for example, frankly regards him as a pagan king.[33] And while Beowulf may well be "brave and gentle, blameless in thought and deed, the king that dies for his people,"[34] he is nevertheless of all men the "most eager for praise," and his actions are always those of the pagan Germanic chieftain rather than those of the "Christian Savior" that Klaeber thought him to be. Beowulf recognizes as binding all the customs and laws of the *comites*, including the obligation of the warrior to avenge himself on his enemies; he undertakes his exploits primarily out of a desire for both glory and gold; his last thoughts are "sad, restless, brooding on death";[35] he feels just before his death that he has somehow angered a vengeful God; and his final wish is to see the treasure hoard he has won. Compared with these fundamental actions and attitudes, his brief thanksgivings to God seem superficial, so much so that J. R. R. Tolkien remarks: "We have in Beowulf's language little differentiation of God and Fate."[36] The much-discussed identification of Grendel with the race of Cain can hardly be called Christian, even though its source is scriptural; it is best taken simply as a means of expanding and intensifying the poet's vision of the evil forces of pagan nature. Moreover, as Klaeber admits, there is no mention at all of the elements of specifically Christian experience such as are found in the religious poems of the period: "We hear nothing of angels, saints, relics, of Christ and the cross, of divine worship, church observances, or any particular dogmatic points."[37]

Its paganism, on the other hand, is essential to the

79

thought and action of *Beowulf*. The externals of paganism—the omens, sacrifices, and burials—are as peripheral as the externals of Christianity. But the great concepts that determine structure and theme—the unmitigated pessimism, the doctrine of an unyielding fate, the poet's insistence upon the obligations of kinship and the vendetta, the praise of worldly heroism, and the glorification of prowess and courage for their own sakes—these are indispensable to any interpretation of *Beowulf*. All these concepts point toward a deep-seated pagan tradition of thought and action which the Christianity of the period, at best syncretic, managed to color but not to erase or disguise.

I suspect that we have fallen into the habit of seeing *Beowulf* as a Christian poem simply because we know more about late medieval Christianity than we do about the Germanic paganism of the Dark Ages. It is far easier to look back at *Beowulf*, Church Fathers in hand, from the Christian vantage point of the late Middle Ages than from the pagan point of view of the earlier centuries, from which so little information has come down. The remnants of paganism that did survive in Britain—the scattered altars, the maimed rites and dances, the denunciations from Rome and local clergy—tell us almost nothing. The precise relationships among the English, German, and Scandinavian mythologies are blurred. The fact that a number of historians fall back upon *Beowulf* itself to "see therein much of the workings of the primitive English mind"[38] demonstrates the scantiness of our information concerning pagan Britain. Whitelock, for example, can be most explicit about the degree of Christian knowledge held by the poet's audience; however, she is of necessity silent concerning that same audience's knowledge of pagan doctrines. Yet whether or not one wishes to accept Murray's theory of a continuing English pagan tradition, one must accept the fact that the audience of *Beowulf* was very close indeed to its pagan heritage and could still understand and appreciate a pagan tale in its own terms, even though the tale might be shaped and rendered respectable by a poet with an eye cocked toward the local clergy.

The essential paganism of the poem, like its distrust of the heroic attitude, is more evident in the second half than in the first. As the tragedy of Beowulf approaches, the poet finds little to say concerning the hero's Christianity and little consolation in the comforting thoughts of its saints. Beowulf dies a lonely death; he finds little solace either in the memory of his accomplishments, which will be of no lasting value to his people, or in the possibility of future glory. And, unlike the authors of the religious poems of the period, neither does the *Beowulf*-poet find solace, though we are assured by the religious references in the poem that he was at least nominally a Christian.

The poem taken as a whole thus advances neither the heroic, the heroic-kingly, nor the Christian ideal as a permanent or wholly satisfactory way of combatting the evils of life and of nature, symbolized in the poem by the monsters, although it does place these concepts in a kind of perspective. In his youth the individual hero may prevail, but sooner or later his strength flags and the code by which he lives cannot provide a stable or lasting government, mankind's best safeguard against evil. The wise king, on the other hand, may for a time maintain the state by sacrificing heroic to corporate values, but, paradoxically, in the end he must turn to the youthful hero for protection; even the king's heroic self-sacrifice cannot save his nation from destruction. And the Christian may practice humility, but this virtue is of little use in combatting the hostile natural forces against which man must contend.

Like the *Iliad* and the *Odyssey, Beowulf* is thus principally concerned with the comparative roles in society of the individual and the ruler, and society itself is seen in relation both to history and to nature. Unlike the Homeric epics, however, *Beowulf*, because of its Scandinavian background, assumes a view of man and nature which is almost totally pessimistic in terms of the fate awaiting both society and the individual. Despite an occasional outcropping of the irrational,[39] the cosmos in Homer is essentially ordered and just. Thus while the lot of an individual or a nation, an

Achilles or a Troy, may be tragic, their tragedies stem from their failure to observe the moral laws which have governed the universe since the beginning of time and which even the more frivolous of the gods cannot suspend.

The universe of Germanic paganism, on the other hand, despite the influence of Christianity, is amoral and chaotic, a battleground between gods and giants. Physical nature, that portion of the battleground inhabited by man, is a fearful den of monsters; and society, symbolized in the poem by the warm, bright meadhall set in the midst of a hostile forest, represents man's only hope of security and survival. The first half of the poem emphasizes the never-ending battle between man and nature in the starkest terms: infuriated by the joy of the hall, the monster attacks and all but destroys the puny civilization that man has created. And the poem as a whole demonstrates clearly enough that despite the efforts of the hero, the king, and the Christian, in the end the meadhall burns and the society is destroyed. No set of values—heroic, kingly, or Christian—can long maintain the state in a universe in which the gods themselves have no power to combat the forces of destruction.

To the Greeks Fate, the Moerae, was essentially a moral concept: Troy will fall because Troy sanctioned Paris's crime; Agamemnon will be punished because Agamemnon sacrificed his daughter to preserve his reputation and his pride. The *Wyrd* that governs *Beowulf*, on the other hand, is simply a manifestation of a negative, pessimistic view of history in which men, nations, and even gods may wrest only a brief hour of personal triumph before succumbing to the overpowering forces bent on their destruction.

This is not to say that *Beowulf* is an amoral poem but simply that its action, despite the Christian elements, takes place against the background of an amoral universe. The ethical standards to which the characters adhere are not imposed on them from above but have been framed by man and hence are more social than religious in nature. Indeed part of the confusion of values from which the hero suffers may result from the poet's unsuccessful attempt to impose the Christian world view upon the pagan. Were the poem wholly Christian in its outlook, the hero would not be concerned with the failure of the *comitatus* code to establish a heaven on earth, choosing instead to concentrate upon his future glory in the true felicity of Heaven. As it stands, having practiced only halfheartedly the humble ways of the Christian, preferring always to be seen as "most eager for praise," he lives in confusion and dies unhappy and disillusioned.

As with the confusion of heroic and kingly values, this imperfect union of pagan and Christian philosophies is perhaps a result of the poet's place in history, his view of the past. Just as the first of his period's two great historical movements, the movement toward unification among the Anglian states of the North, threw doubts upon the efficacy of the *comitatus* code without firmly establishing a workable alternative, so the second, the conversion of England to Christianity, succeeded in its early stages in disestablishing paganism without wholly discrediting it. *Beowulf*, we must remember, was written within seventy-five years of the Synod of Whitby, and just as there is ample contemporaneous evidence that pagan altars still flourished in England, so the confusion of religious values in *Beowulf* demonstrates that pagan ideas continued as well.

It is also instructive that in *Beowulf*, as in the *Iliad* and the *Odyssey*, the characters who represent most clearly the values of hero and king are drawn respectively from myth and history. Although only one event, Hygelac's raid against the Frisians, can be positively authenticated and dated, nevertheless the fact that "the *Beowulf* narrative is fully confirmed by the unquestioned accounts of early chroniclers, coupled with the comparative nearness of the poem to the time of the events recounted, raises into probability the belief that we are dealing in the main with fairly authentic narrative."[40] Certainly "the accounts of early chroniclers" point to the historical reality of Hrothgar, for example, despite the poet's inconsistencies in dealing with his age and reign.

Beowulf, on the other hand, seems a creation of legend and myth. His encounters with the monsters have analogs in folktales throughout the North, and his physical attributes, particularly his strength, seem more godlike than human. Moreover, his place in the Geatish royal genealogy seems fabricated since his name does not alliterate with those of the Geatish kings, which all begin with H, nor with those of his supposed father, Ecgtheow, or his family, the Waegmundings. Like Achilles, he is a solitary figure: he takes little part in the known historical actions of the time, his long and peaceful reign corresponds to no known historical period, and he dies without offspring.

Hrothgar, the historical king, and Beowulf, the mythical hero, hold in very general terms in the first half of the poem the positions held by Agamemnon and Achilles in the *Iliad*, though of course the Germanic heroes are not engaged in personal conflict but are simply faced with the same problem. Furthermore, Beowulf makes the same transition from hero to king that Odysseus accomplishes so brilliantly in the *Odyssey*. However, though the device of amalgamation serves the same literary purpose in the Greek and Anglo-Saxon poems, that is, to give emphasis and meaning to history and literary credibility to myth, the differences in the use of history and myth by the two poets are perhaps more significant than the similarities, the variations more meaningful than the pattern. For the Greek epics end not in tragedy but in at least a modified triumph. Achilles is cured of his heroic madness, and Agamemnon comes at last to understand the responsibilities of kingship; but Beowulf in his heroic pride attacks the firedrake alone and dies embittered by his failures, and Hrothgar in his decrepitude helplessly presides over the destruction of his kingdom by both natural and human enemies. Odysseus is able to substitute a nonheroic standard of expediency for the heroic rashness of his early days and so restore Ithaca to peace and stability; but Beowulf, despite his long rule, is never quite able to understand the corporate nature of kingship and so cannot make provisions for the future welfare of his nation.

Much of the pessimistic spirit of *Beowulf* is probably attributable to those bits of history and legend which the poet inherited from the oral tradition, material which he could shape to his own devices but which he could not radically alter. Certainly the histories of the Scandinavian tribes known by the poet were marked by tales of their rapid rise and fall, and Germanic myth and legend are unremittingly tragic from creation to doomsday.

Thus *Beowulf* was composed under historical conditions strikingly like those which contributed to the composition of the Homeric poems—the heroic age of the past, the oral tradition, the new society and religion of the poet's own age, the genius of a poet able to place past and present in a new perspective; it deals with almost precisely the same themes —the relation of heroic to kingly values and of the individual to society—and uses the same kind of formulaic language, the same basic character types, and the same amalgamation of myth, legend, and history. Nevertheless, *Beowulf* presents a far different picture of man, nature, and society from that of the *Iliad* and the *Odyssey*. The pessimism of *Beowulf* has, as I have suggested, a number of causes: society in the poet's time had outgrown the *comitatus* code but had evolved only the haziest beginnings of a concept of kingship that could assure a stable government; the negative pagan philosophy of nature and history still strongly permeated the thinking of the age, despite the softening effects of Christianity; and the primitive legend and historical accounts inherited by the poet through the oral tradition were basically tragic. The poem ends in tragedy and disillusionment because the poet sees no alternative either in the past or in his own time. That *Beowulf* is a poem about heroism is indisputable, as is the fact that the poet everywhere praises the hero's glorious victories, but it does not therefore follow, as many critics assume, that the poem wholeheartedly advocates the heroic way of life. It is all very well to say, as does Wrenn, that "a Germanic hero is a tragic hero, who shows his highest greatness not alone in winning glory by victory, but rather by finding his supremely noble qualities in the moment of death in battle";[41] but *Beowulf* as a whole demonstrates that the poet, looking back along his corridor in time, did not find it so. Heroism, the poet seems to say, is fine and glorious for the youth who is both strong and lucky, but it brings little aid and comfort to the aged king faced with the inevitable annihilation of self and nation.

I would suggest that the pagan archetype of the poem, or at least the folk elements from which it sprang, and the harsh realities of Anglo-Saxon political life eventually dominate the mood and theme of *Beowulf* and that the pessimism of Nordic mythology finally overshadows whatever brighter Christian colors the poem initially displays. Beowulf is finally revealed not as a heroic Christian ruler whose life of noble victories and sacrificial death have advanced the cause of God or civilization but as an old king who, though permitted by Fate to win with the help of the young his last battle, nevertheless dies knowing that he has accomplished nothing of permanent value. And in this regard, as we shall see, Beowulf is far closer to the heroes of the medieval epics that are obviously more pagan than Christian—the *Nibelungenlied* and *Njals saga*, for example—than to those of such patently Christian poems as the *Chanson de Roland*. For although the *Nibelungenlied* and *Njals saga* were presumably written by Christian poets, their heroes are essentially pagan. Gunnar and Njal, Siegfried and Rudiger perish as the result of feuds that are in the end as meaningless as they are futile. They do not die on behalf of noble causes, nor do they really serve their parties' best interests by dying, however well they die. Scandinavian mythology presents a negative, pessimistic view of history in which all men, living and dead, and earth and giants are to participate and be destroyed in the final act of a conflict with the gods. Although a new heaven and earth may eventually arise from the ashes of the old, the present life of man is marked not only by struggle but also by a sense of the futility of struggle. And to this sense of futility *Beowulf*, despite its heroic form and tone, finally succumbs.

CHAPTER FOUR

The Song of Roland

One would think that since the historical incident which underlies the *Song of Roland* is comparatively well documented the problem of tracing the development of the story from history to epic would be a far easier task than in those poems, the *Iliad* and the *Odyssey,* for example, where the exact circumstances of their historical antecedents have been forever lost. Yet such is not the case. Largely through the debates of scholars, the problem of the means of transmission of the Roland legend has come to obscure the relationship between the poem and its sources to such an extent that any discussion of the poem seemingly must involve itself with the great battle between "traditionalists" and "individualists." Thus we have lost sight of the simple fact that, however and through whatever agencies the legend may have evolved during the three hundred years which separate battle and poem, we do have in our possession here, as nowhere else in heroic literature, both fact and fiction and so are able to see at least the beginning and the ending of the process by which that literature is created.

The beginning is simple enough. According to the chronicler Einhard, writing about 820, the rearguard and baggage train of Charlemagne's army, returning from a brief and apparently unsuccessful summer campaign in Spain, were ambushed and attacked by a group of Basque marauders in the densely wooded pass at Roncevaux in the Pyrenees. The Basques, Einhard says, had disposed their forces along the heights and had swept down suddenly on the French forces, killing them to a man and escaping under cover of darkness with the baggage. Among those killed, he adds, were "Eggihard the king's seneschal, Anselm, Count of the Palace, and Roland, warden of the Marches of Brittany, together with a great many others." The date we know—August 15, 778.

A great deal has been made of Einhard's account. There is little doubt that he attempts to whitewash the Spanish campaign. Although the combined French and Moorish armies had made prior agreements with Suleiman, the Moorish (and hence pagan) governor of Barcelona, to rid Spain of the last member of the Umayyad dynasty, Abdur Rahman, they failed to take Saragossa, their principal objective. Aside from a few minor victories, Charlemagne had little to show for what must have been a considerable military effort; faced with a shortage of supplies and the threat of renewed Saxon attacks at home, he decided to cut his losses and return to France almost emptyhanded.

It may be also that the ambush itself was no minor skirmish. In the second version of *Annales Royales,* once also attributed to Einhard, the chronicler relates that the Basque attack threw the whole French army into turmoil and that Charlemagne's main force suffered major losses.

But too much can be made of the actual circumstances of the battle. Certainly its historical outcome is of no importance to the poem. In the poem it becomes both defeat and victory, a last-ditch effort and a heroic, though tragic, defeat followed by a smashing revenge. It is the way of the heroic imagination thus to turn both victory and defeat into poetic truth. Indeed, the greatest "real-life" heroes of the Western tradition have been the noble failures, those who died well—Scott in Antarctica, Mallory on Everest, the Light Brigade, Crockett at the Alamo, Custer at Little Big Horn. And what reader does not honestly prefer Hector to Achilles?

Whatever the exact circumstances of the battle of Roncevaux, the *Song of Roland* as it exists in its most finished form, that of the so-called Oxford version, dates from a much later time, the late eleventh or early twelfth century. The other extant versions of the tale—a twelfth-century German translation, a thirteenth-century Norse version, a

Franco-Venetian assonanced text, the Latin prose *Pseudo-Turpin* which is a part of the pilgrim's guide to the shrine of Saint James at Compestella, the *Carmen de prodicione Guenonis,* also in Latin prose—are all later than the Oxford text. However, according to William of Malmesbury some version of the legend was chanted by the Norman *jongleur* Taillefer at Hastings in 1066, and the newly discovered *Nota Emilianense,* which is possibly as early as 1065, contains a reference to the death of Roland. Even so, the *Song of Roland* in the Oxford text is not only the finest version of the poem but also the most primitive.

It is this fact more than any other that has led scholars to dispute the origins of the poem as we have it. For not only are there no clear sources for the poem, there are no documents whatsoever by which the evolution of the story can be traced from the battle of Roncevaux in 778 to its reemergence in heroic song in the early twelfth century. The two major alternatives are thus that the story existed in a continuous or nearly continuous oral tradition prior to its appearance in the poem—the position of the traditionalists—or that the poem is entirely the inspired creation of its author, who is himself responsible for its form and matter, including its remarkable transformation of history into legend—the position of the individualists.

There are, of course, arguments on both sides.[1] Among the traditionalists, the celebrated French scholar Gaston Paris believed that the *chansons de geste,* of which the *Song of Roland* is very nearly the first and certainly the best example, were descended from *cantilenae,* Old French songs dealing with heroes of the past; and Pio Rajna pointed out that since there are a number of German epics dating from the Carolingian period there could well have been similar French poems, now lost, by means of which the story was transmitted, especially since these Germanic epics and the *chansons de geste* share a number of motifs, particularly the naming of swords and horses, the common occurrence of the number twelve, the fact that the king seeks advice from his nobles, and the use of giants and monsters. More recent writers have suggested other ways in which the legend of Roncevaux may have been kept alive—in Latin epic, anecdotal, and hagiographical works; in a purely oral poetic tradition such as that which Homer inherited; or even in prose sagas descended from eyewitness accounts. And, of course, the *Song of Roland* itself refers to an older work, a *geste Francor,* and Einhard in the *Vita Caroli* records that Charlemagne himself ordered written down a number of *barbara et antquissima carmina quibus veterum regum actus et bella canebantur.* There is also evidence that the so-called *Pseudo-Turpin,* though composed at a later date than the *Song of Roland,* contains vestiges of an earlier poem written in Latin hexameters, and there are frequent examples as early as 1040 of children being baptized Roland and Oliver, presumably in honor of already famous heroes. Most noteworthy perhaps is the evidence of the Spanish *Nota Emilianense* that the legend of Roncevaux, along with a number of the other Charlemagne stories, was in existence as early as 1065.

The case made against the traditionalists by the individualists rests upon the fact that there simply are no clear sources for the poem and that there is very little evidence, and that of a very doubtful nature, for the existence of the legend before the mid-eleventh century. Neither is there any assurance that the *carmina* to which Einhard refers or the various Latin saints' lives of the period dealt with the Roland legend or that any oral tradition dating as far back as the Carolingian period could have been maintained through the confused, chaotic days of the tenth century.

Thus the individualists, following the general theory laid down by Joseph Bédier, have insisted that the *chansons de geste* are in every way products of the age in which they were written and that they are the creations of individual authors who manufactured heroic literature without access to a continuous oral tradition or to lost heroic epics. Bédier maintained that the *chansons de geste* were a natural expression of the crusading fervor of the eleventh century and that their authors drew their inspiration and materials from local traditions and perhaps from chronicles preserved in monasteries located along the great pilgrim routes. Thus the *jongleur* learns from monks along the pilgrim route to the shrine of Saint James of Compestella of the great battle which took place in these very mountains; he is shown relics of the battle and perhaps even chronicles which record the heroic deaths of Roland, Oliver, and Archbishop Turpin. Moved by them and by the sight of the landscape before him, the *jongleur* re-creates the battle in an imaginative poem which embraces not only what he has heard and seen but also what he imagines and infers from the monks' story, that the battle must have been a part of the great struggle between Cross and Crescent in which his whole world is now involved. As Jan de Vries points out, *Poeta vindicatus* might well be the title of "Bédier's fascinating argument."[2] For while later theorists have modified Bédier's theory deemphasizing the importance of the monasteries in the preservation of the legend, and while there have been attempts to bridge the gap between the two schools, the individualists have held fast to the belief that the *Song of Roland,* like the later *chansons de geste,* is the work of a single poet who inherited only the scantiest raw materials from which he single-handedly created a noble work of art.

As I have said, one can dwell too long on this question of origin and so come to ignore the evidence that we do have, the *chansons de geste* themselves. And while no one would willingly dare to attack the fortifications of the Bédierists without fresh ammunition, I do think it possible to maintain, particularly from the evidence supplied by the poems themselves, that the *Song of Roland* manifests some remnants of its origin in oral tradition and that its author—like Homer, a man of genius—was working within an established literary form.

First of all, the various studies made of the earliest *chansons,* particularly those in the William of Orange cycle, demonstrate, despite Bédier's objections, that a number of traditions centering around such popular figures as the eighth-century Guillaume de Toulouse did indeed survive the dark days of the tenth century by means other than monkish chronicles. Even the fragmentary *Gormont and Isembart,* which may well have been the first composed of the *chansons de geste,* shares a number of features with the *Song of Roland:* it is written in verse stanzas called *laisses,* though of the older eight-syllable variety, which have unequal numbers of verses linked by assonance; its plot centers about the treachery of knight to king; it concentrates upon the "personal human tragedy"[3] of the action rather than simply its externals. And even though Bédier claimed that the genesis of the poem might be found in the local traditions of the Abbey of Saint-Riquier, other equally astute scholars, notably Albert Pauphilet and Ferdinand Lot, have seen in it remnants of a ninth- or tenth-century Norman saga.

The *Song of William,* discovered in 1903 and dating back to the late eleventh century, is evidence of a continuing epic tradition concerning Guillaume de Toulouse before the eleventh century. Like those of the *Song of Roland,* many of its *laisses,* written in the assonated ten-syllable line, have a refrain. Here we have a king and his proud warrior-nephew who makes a last-minute appeal to the king for help and dies in battle. As Urban Holmes says, the style of the poem is "cruder than that of *Roland,*" and "its psychology is more primitive."[4]

More important, however, is the fact that the *Song of William* presupposes, as do the Homeric epics and *Beowulf,* a prior knowledge of the legend on the part of its listeners. The characters of William's nephew Vivien, his wife Guibourc, and the giant Reneward all play roles in the later poems of the cycle, and in relating the incident of Vivien's death the poet not only does not feel compelled to identify these characters in detail but also treats them in the same spirit as do the other poets in the tradition: Vivien is heroic, Guibourc energetic, Reneward both fierce and comic. And indeed there is in all the poems of the William of Orange cycle a notable consistency of character and incident. The so-called *Hague Fragment,* which may be as early as the late tenth century, mentions a number of the characters made familiar by the William cycle. Since this fragment is generally thought to be a "prose rendering of a Latin epic, which in turn was translated from a vernacular *chanson de geste*,"[5] it too bears clear witness to a tradition far older than itself.

We are thus able to see in these early pieces vestiges of an older tradition which, while undoubtedly reflecting, as Bédier insisted, monastic influence in transmission, is nevertheless for the most part heroic rather than religious; warriors far outnumber saints and battles miracles in these poems. And although the exact steps by which the French epic tradition developed cannot be traced, it would seem to bear a close resemblance to those which produced the Homeric epics and *Beowulf*. One can, of course, go too far in speculating upon the nature of a tradition for which there is no extant evidence; but analogy, despite its misuse, is a legitimate tool of literary criticism, and even the "purest" speculation can illuminate areas whose darkness more scientific devices cannot pierce.

There is present in these poems, for example, the same fusion of legend and myth and history we have observed elsewhere. Guillaume de Toulouse did in fact live in the eighth century, and the battle of Saucourt against the Vikings, the central event of *Gormont and Isembart*, was an actual event of 881. However, the historical William certainly did not possess the sword of Charlemagne, *Joyeuse*, the creation of a mythical dwarf; nor was his wife, Guibourc, a captured Saracen princess. Nor was the battle against the Saracens which forms the central episode of the *Song of William* won by a gigantic kitchen knave armed with a club.

The *Song of Roland* itself illustrates the process of fusion very well. At the time of the battle of Roncevaux the emperor was thirty-six years old; he is in the poem a patriarchal figure well over two hundred years of age. Since so great a king would naturally rule over a court of great magnificence, legend has created for him the twelve peers of French chivalry, headed by Roland, who is no longer simply warden of the Breton Marches but Charlemagne's nephew and the

93

conqueror of "Noples and Commibles . . . , Valterne and the country of Pine, and Balasgued and Tuele and Sezile."[6] Charlemagne's brief and probably disastrous Spanish summer campaign has become a brilliant seven years' conquest. Most interesting perhaps is that the small band of Basque marauders has been replaced by half a million Saracens, thus not only placing the battle within the context of the Crusades but also providing the French heroes with opponents worthy of their steel. It would be unthinkable, moreover, that the twelve peers could be defeated in fair battle even by such opponents, so the element of treachery has been added and the peers' deaths avenged by Charlemagne's victory over Baligant.

It seems evident, coming from a study of the Homeric epics and *Beowulf*, that while the *Roland*-poet may very well have added a number of details—particularly, I would guess, the passages dealing with the "relics," Roland's sword and horn—as well as a new thematic emphasis, the sweeping changes from fact to legend represent the increments of time upon circumstance. Given evidence in neither direction, it seems to me that (to follow the principle of Ockham's Razor) the theory of a developing heroic oral tradition centering around figures such as Roland and William of Orange best explains the form and content of the *chansons de geste*.

For example, the *Song of Roland* makes no effort, with one exception, to introduce its major characters, a practice which, as C. M. Bowra says concerning the *Iliad*, demonstrates that "the poet composed for listeners who knew of his characters and their histories."[7] "Charles the king, our great emperor, has stayed seven full years in Spain and has conquered that proud land right up to the sea," the poem begins and then plunges into the council of Marsiliun, the pagan king of Saragossa. Roland is first mentioned toward the end of the list of Charlemagne's barons and is not particularly identified when he begins to speak. True, he begins his statement by listing his principal conquests, but his boasting here seems more to establish his character than his identity.

Only Oliver, for reasons we shall explore later, is insistently identified in these opening verses.

It has been demonstrated, moreover, that there are present in the *chansons de geste* epic formulas,[8] a fact that indicates, again as in the Homeric epics, the existence of an inherited oral poetic tradition. Indeed, the *laisses similaires,* the repeated triads of stanzas for which the *Song of Roland* is noted, may be evidence of the poet's conscious adaptation of a traditional oral formula to a particular literary need, that of extending climactic moments by repeating with varying emphases and the addition of detail such vital points as Ganelon's betrayal and Roland's decision to refrain from blowing the horn. Again, the word *AOI,* which follows a number of *laisses,* is generally agreed to be a refrain, possibly shouted by singer and audience together, and so may be a vestige of an oral tradition stretching back into the Carolingian age.

I would maintain also that the theme and structure of the *Song of Roland* reflect its origin in oral tradition. Although there are myriad statements to the effect that the *chansons de geste* deal with "the social, religious, moral, and imaginative conditions of the epoch which produced them; and that that epoch begins in the eleventh century,"[9] it may well be that there remain in the poem vestiges of the age which produced the legend as well as vestiges of the poet's age—again as in the *Iliad,* the *Odyssey,* and *Beowulf.*

French history from the death of Charlemagne in 814 to the end of the eleventh century was a period of continuing crisis and confusion marked by the collapse of the post-Carolingian kingdoms and the rise of feudalism. There can be little doubt that the French dynasty beginning with the early mayors of the palace and culminating in Charles Martel, Pippin, and finally Charlemagne was politically far ahead of its time in establishing for Europe a common rule and civilization. This it accomplished largely through a skillful use of the one organization common to all Europeans, the Church. By encouraging missions, establishing the parish system in rural areas, and creating a unifying myth, the Holy

95

Roman Empire, to which all Europeans might subscribe, the Carolingian kings were able to overcome, at least for a time, the regional differences which divided the continent and to gather into a single office the major strands of legislative power.

But Carolingian rule could not impose on Europe any sort of economic unity. Communications were slow and untrustworthy, trade between distant cities almost impossible. Thus the progeny of Charlemagne, unfortunately men of no great ability, found it impossible to exact any real influence over local authorities. Unfortunately also, the three grandchildren of Charlemagne divided among them the great empire, thus creating what would in time become the modern states of France and Germany as well as a middle kingdom which itself quickly divided into a number of small warring states. The political confusion caused by the ensuing petty wars was increased, moreover, by the fact that the local lord had also to defend his lands against the predatory raids of the Vikings, Magyars, and Saracens, a task no central government could do for him.

The chief result of the disintegration of the post-Carolingian kingdoms in the ninth century was the emergence of feudalism. As historians have pointed out, the spread of feudalism was not in any way planned; indeed it could hardly be called a "system" of government in any modern sense of the term. It was at best a makeshift scheme, the roots of which extended well back into the Germanic *comites* of pre-Carolingian times, which provided a means of order in a period of threatening chaos stemming from the failure of central government and from the outside attacks. Its chief feature was the mutual responsibility of lord and vassal in a continuous and flexible chain of authority. The vassal, largely autonomous in the governing of his own domain, was obliged to furnish his lord with military service; furthermore, although he was not, as in the *comites*, a member of his lord's household, he owed to him the same sort of personal, as opposed to national, loyalty we have observed in the early Germanic societies. The lord, in turn, guaranteed to his supporters protection, justice, and an adequate reward for their services.

Under Charlemagne feudalism was perfectly compatible with the idea of a unified government and, indeed, during the Dark Ages that followed, men still spoke of empires. But during the unsettled days of the tenth century there was nothing that approached, except in name, a feeling for or loyalty to anything above the personal allegiance to a local lord. However, as feudalism developed, particularly through the granting of pieces of land called fiefs in return for services granted a lord, it began to grow more complex and hence more centralized. As his kingdom extended, the feudal lord became more unwilling to leave his vassals completely autonomous in governing their provinces and so created deputies to check the power of his subordinates. And as commerce and industry increased throughout Europe during the eleventh century, the feudal system, which was based on a purely agrarian economy, began to lose control of a serf population which was moving from village to town and could now demand, and receive, more for its services than mere protection. Finally, the religious revival which swept Europe as a result of the Saracen assaults on the holy places of the East did much to bring Europeans together in a cause which transcended their local interests and allegiances.

Hence the rise in authority and power of the Capetian kings in France can be attributed largely to their ability to preserve in even the most troubled times the vestiges of royal authority, and to their good fortune in preserving a direct line of descent. To be sure, by the end of the eleventh century, the time of the writing of the *Song of Roland*, France was still ruled for the most part by its great dukes. Even so, the dukedoms of Flanders and Normandy, indeed most of the northern dukedoms, were stable and free from violence and had in fact become feudal states rather than simply feudal lordships. The officers of these dukes were able to supervise the courts and financial interests of their masters and so protect them from rebellious vassals. At every level, then, the decentralized feudalism of earlier centuries had faded, the power of the crown was steadily increasing, and the institutions and indeed the political thought of the West, even within the great dukedoms, had developed far beyond the simple personal loyalties of early feudalism. It was not long before an allegiance to France replaced allegiance to Normandy or Flanders.

By the mid-twelfth century Europe had been reshaped by the emergence of a new culture based on new customs and institutions; one can see everywhere the brilliant effects of new learning, new manners, even, in courtly love, a new relation between men and women. Chivalry emerged from knighthood just as monarchy emerged from feudalism. And although, as I have said, the vast majority of critics see in the *Song of Roland* the "social, religious, moral, and imaginative conditions" of this new era, it is also possible to find in its action and ethos remnants of late Carolingian and early Capetian times, of the three hundred years of feudal confusion during which the memory of Roncevaux was preserved, probably in both *cantilenae* and narrative lays, in the courts of warlords throughout France. Indeed the very diffusion of the legend seems to point to some such conclusion: evidence of a form of the name "Oliver" indicates a "powerful and certainly poetic Roland tradition in the Anjou area"[10] by the mid-eleventh century, while the *Nota Emilianense* from the same period reflects the popularity of the legend in the south of France.

In fact, like the Homeric epics and *Beowulf*, the poem contains a mixture of political and social ideas and, like those poems, sees the values of its own time as essentially opposed to those of the more heroic age which it ostensibly celebrates. This contrast between the personalized feudalism of the past and the rising spirit of loyalty to crown and nation is expressed in a number of ways, particularly in the clear-cut opposition in values, upon which the poet insists, between Roland and Oliver.

"Roland is proud [*proz*] and Oliver is wise [*sage*]," the poet says (l. 1093), and their actions plainly bear out this description. They are most conspicuously contrasted in the two horn-blowing episodes, the first of which centers upon Roland's refusal to summon Charlemagne at the beginning of the battle and the second on his final decision, the battle being lost, to call the emperor so that the rearguard's defeat may be avenged. The first episode occupies eight full *laisses*. *Laisses* 80–82 recount Oliver's description of the pagan host; *laisses* 83–86, Oliver's plea to Roland to summon Charlemagne's host and Roland's proud refusal; and *laisse* 87, after the statement that "Roland is proud and Oliver is wise," Oliver's reproach to Roland: "You would not sound your horn for pride; . . . now whoever fights today will never fight again" (ll. 1101–5).

Like most of the *laisses similaires,* these are incremental, each extending the implications of the total situation. *Laisse* 80 begins with Oliver's climbing a hill to survey the enemy host, whose presence has been announced by trumpets. Oliver's reconnoitering of the enemy forces is, of course, an indication of his prudent, practical nature, but, more important, it allows him to come to two immediate conclusions about the situation, neither of which the proud Roland will accept—that they have been betrayed by Ganelon and that they cannot win the battle. Both of these conclusions are rejected by Roland on the same grounds, personal honor and family pride. He cannot conceive that his stepfather, however much they may disagree within the family, could ever betray the French; and he positively ignores the second warning, his whole concern being with his own conduct in the battle rather than the welfare of the army he commands or its chances of victory.

The wise Oliver, having failed to dissuade Roland from battle, now suggests that Roland blow the olifant to summon Charlemagne and thus insure a French victory. But Roland refuses even this sage advice, again arguing that such conduct would bring dishonor to him and his family forever. Instead he eagerly anticipates the approaching battle, not because it will advance the cause of France or even of Christianity but because it will give him an opportunity to enhance his own reputation. Like Hotspur, whom he greatly resem-

99

bles, Roland becomes more eager for battle with the news that his force is outnumbered. It is indeed a discouraged Oliver who accuses Roland of sacrificing an army for pride.

The second of the horn-blowing episodes presents a startling contrast to the first. As long as the tide of battle had favored the French, Roland had remained gleeful, urging his men on and boasting over the slain enemy. But now only sixty of the original twenty thousand Frenchmen remain alive, and the hero is suddenly appalled by the consequences of his first decision. Turning to Oliver, he asks naively why the emperor has not come to aid them and how he may yet summon him.

Oliver's reactions to Roland's late decision to blow the olifant have, it seems to me, been generally misinterpreted. It seems unreasonable that the poet, having insisted on Oliver's prudence and concern for others in the earlier incident, would here present him as an image of stubborn pride. True, Oliver may feel that since their cause is past praying for, personal honor is all that is now left to the French survivors; and there is also something of an "I told you so" tone in his speech. But Oliver in answering Roland echoes almost explicitly the hero's former arguments: they will lose renown and their families will be disgraced if they sound the horn in defeat. Oliver's remarks in this crucial scene are thus consistently and cynically ironic, bitterly mimicking Roland's earlier vaunts; as Roland says, the words are spoken bitterly and in anger. But this is the natural reaction of a man of good will and common sense who has seen an impulsive, irresponsible fool destroy himself and others for the sake of an ill-thought-out set of slogans. Little wonder that Oliver wishes to renounce the chivalric ties, closer even than blood ties, which have bound the warriors since boyhood and that he proclaims Roland unfit to marry his sister. And against this withering attack Roland can defend himself only with a pitiful rationalization—"I have struck many strong blows"—and with a childish attempt, now that it is too late, to repair the irreparable damage—"I will blow the horn and King Charles will hear."

But there is more in Oliver's words here than pique at Roland or bitterness at the inevitability of his own death. His final and longest speech, *laisse* 131, abandons the biting irony of the preceding *laisses* to give plain voice to the real cause of his renunciation of Roland and the values Roland represents:

> There is prudent courage, and there is foolhardiness. These French are dead because of your recklessness, and we will never give service for Charles again. If you had heeded me, my lord would have come, we would have won this battle, and King Marsiliun would have been taken or killed. Your prowess, Roland, has proved our undoing. We will never again come to the aid of Charles the Great, a man whose greatness will never be excelled. You will die here and France will be humbled. Now has our loyal companionship been broken, and before nightfall we will have parted in grief. (ll. 1725–35)

In substituting rashness for prudent courage, the hero has destroyed not only himself, the *douze* peers, and the rearguard but the cause of France as well: "You will die here," Oliver says, but more important, "France will be humbled." And it is certainly significant that Archbishop Turpin immediately joins the discussion with the argument that, if summoned, Charles can at least avenge their deaths and procure a national victory.

The contrast in values that separates Roland and Oliver is thus not simply a matter of pride versus prudence but rather individualistic, irresponsible, chivalric pride, the outlook of the tenth-century feudal aristocracy, against the considered, though nonetheless courageous, and at least partly nationalistic prudence of the new age of the Capetian kings. It is certainly clear that Roland's attitude is typically feudal. He regards the rearguard as his vassals, loyal to him personally and subject to his every demand, presumably by virtue of his specific commission by Charlemagne. He is motivated by the desire for personal glory; he cannot endure the thought of personal and family shame. In short, he recognizes no allegiance to any authority except that based on a purely personal commitment. Moreover, Roland's famous *doel* (l. 1867), the powerful emotion with which he views at the very end of the battle the slaughtered French around him, is clearly, as George Fenwick Jones says, "chagrin" rather than "grief" in any Christian sense; it is the despondency into which a feudal hero falls upon realizing "that he will lose his honor because of his defeat and his inability to protect his men."[11] Significantly, in this same *laisse* (140) he refers to his men as "vassals" and states that they died for his sake, thus emphasizing even here his feudal point of view toward them.

Oliver, on the other hand, is always motivated by a sense of responsibility toward his nation. Whereas Roland always approaches an issue in terms only of personalities (his whimsical and gleeful nomination of Ganelon to head the embassy to Marsiliun, for example), Oliver always considers the nation. He greets Roland's offer to go as emissary to Marsiliun with a statement to the effect that the tactless Roland would fail the mission by provoking a quarrel. He himself then volunteers but significantly prefaces his offer with "if the king wishes," a meaningful courtesy which Roland had ignored. We have already observed his careful scouting of the enemy forces, his plea to Roland to recall the main force in order to insure a French victory, and his subsequent bitterness that France should suffer because of Roland's pride.

It is clear that the poet takes special pains to establish the reputation of Oliver as nearly, if not wholly, equal to that of Roland. Although the sources are not available, I think it safe to assume that in the legend as the poet received it Roland was the unqualified hero and Oliver simply his companion. The poet, therefore, may well be responsible for the special attention devoted to Oliver at every opportunity, a treatment which serves to emphasize and elevate the character, and hence the values, of Oliver to an eminence equal to those of Roland. For example, when the names of the two heroes are linked in the early sections of the poem, Oliver's name is nearly always qualified while Roland's is not. When his name is first mentioned, he is "good, noble Oliver" (1. 176); Ganelon, who consistently degrades Roland as foolish and prideful, refers four times to Oliver, in *laisses similaires* to be sure, as a brave, courtly knight (ll. 546, 559, 576, 585). At nearly every opportunity, even in the most casual reference, Oliver is singled out for praise, whereas the name of Roland is left unqualified. (Presumably, of course, Roland's character was already well established.) This treatment calls attention to the differences in values which separate the two heroes and gives weight to Oliver's point of view. It is a matter of the greatest significance also that in the end Oliver completely renounces the bond of companionship that has united the two heroes throughout their lives. In doing so, he is in fact refuting a personal, and hence feudal, oath of loyalty to Roland, not only because it will result in his own death but also because he has seen that any civilization governed by such oaths is capable of foolishly destroying itself.

This same difference between the personal loyalties of feudalism and the national concerns of a later age may also be observed in the trial of Ganelon, which concludes the poem. Ganelon's defense is based upon a sophistry inherent in the feudal code: injuries to personal honor among nobles may be avenged in a political vacuum without affecting the state to which they all owe allegiance. Thus Ganelon does not deny the fact that he provided Marsiliun with vital information concerning Charlemagne's route of march, but he insists that his action was entirely a family affair: "Roland tricked me out of gold and possessions," he says, "and for this I sought his ruin and death. But I will not concede treachery" (ll. 3758–60). Later he adds that in accomplishing his revenge, he was not treasonous.

With such a defense Charlemagne's barons agree. Ganelon's appeal is perfectly valid in feudal terms and the great lords vote for his acquittal. To them it has indeed been a family affair, and Ganelon has acted within his rights in taking revenge on a man who has tarnished his personal honor. That twenty thousand Frenchmen, including the twelve peers, have been slaughtered as a consequence is apparently of little concern to them. His revenge accomplished, Ganelon will now serve the king with love and faith; the barons add that the death of Ganelon will not restore the life of Roland.

Only the knight Thierry comes forward to defend the cause of the grief-stricken king, and his reasons for doing so are instructive. Regardless of Ganelon's relationship with Roland, Thierry argues, the fact that Roland was Charles's officer rendered him sacred. Thus an offense against the king's representative can never be interpreted simply as an attack upon an individual because it is in fact a crime against the state. To be sure, Thierry must settle the issue by personal combat, according to feudal law, but his argument demonstrates clearly the contrast of feudal and national values imposed on the legend by the poet.

The repetition of this major theme in the trial of Ganelon may also help to explain the structure of the poem. Clearly the *Song of Roland* is no casual anthology of episodes; its careful tripartite structure is evidence of the work of a poet conscious of the artistic problems before him. The opening third of the poem deals with Ganelon's treachery; its scenes in the courts of Blancandrin and Charlemagne are set in contrast. The great middle section of the poem, the battle of Roncevaux itself, is carefully structured. It is introduced by the first prophetic visions of Charlemagne, that of Ganelon and the lance and that of the boar, leopard, and boarhound; by the preparations for battle, including the deliberate paralleling of the French and Saracen peers; and by the first incident of the horn. The first part of the battle itself consists of a series of hand-to-hand combats between the peers of both armies in which the pagans are roundly defeated while none of the French peers is lost. There follows a transition passage in which both Charlemagne and the elements are seen lamenting those Frenchmen who will soon die.

The second battle scene follows, and here the tide turns: despite the heroism of the French, their ranks are reduced from twenty thousand to sixty, and six of the peers are slain. At this point occurs the second of the two horn incidents, followed by Charlemagne's decision to turn back to Roncevaux. In the last of the three central battle scenes the French are finally defeated by the Saracen host, the major heroes die, and Charlemagne returns to the battlefield to mourn the slaughter. Charlemagne's lament, his defeat of the remains of Marsiliun's army, and the arrival of Baligant form a natural transition to the final third of the poem, which recounts the battle with Baligant's forces and the trial of Ganelon.

The final episodes have often been thought to be spurious, late additions to both legend and poem. Certainly one's interest tends to flag after the death of Roland. Yet it may well be that the Baligant and Ganelon episodes are as crucial to the action and meaning of the poem, and hence to its structure, as anything that precedes them. The victory over Baligant avenges the deaths of Roland and the rearguard, and the trial of Ganelon completes the action begun with the first lines of the poem. Both are thus necessary to the action of the poem: the deaths of heroes must be avenged and traitors cannot go unpunished.

But this final third of the action (actually almost half the length of the poem) does more than simply provide a denouement. As we have seen, the trial of Ganelon is concerned with the contrast of private and corporate values which so sharply distinguishes Roland from Oliver. It may therefore be that the Baligant episode is introduced not only to provide a fitting vengeance for Roncevaux but also to emphasize the theme of nationalism.

Internationalism, really; or perhaps the whole Church Militant. For suddenly we are no longer dealing simply with the French of the rearguard or the Spanish of Marsiliun's army. Over and over the poet sounds the rollcall and Christian Europe responds; Franks, Bavarians, Normans, Germans, Bretons, Flemings all fight together. And on the other side the whole pagan world is involved; Syrians, Persians, Armenians, and Moors are among the thirty battalions led by Baligant.

The poem thus opens out in the end, and we move from chivalric battle in which man fights man for glory to the world conflict of Cross and Crescent. At last emperor faces emir, archetype against archetype, each more myth than man; but no longer, as at Roncevaux, does mere chivalric prowess or feudal pride settle the issue. Charlemagne's skull is laid bare by Baligant's blows and the emperor staggers. Suddenly Gabriel is at his side, rebuking his weakness: "Great King," the harsh voice demands, "what are you about?" (l. 3611). And Charlemagne arises to strike for God the final blow.

Thus the *Song of Roland,* like the other poems we have examined, exhibits a contrast between the individualistic ideal of a heroic society and the corporate values of a later, more organized society. Whatever its first form, the legend of Roland shows its origins in the age of feudalism; its great hero recognizes no values or ties beyond those of personal commitment to an overlord. Like Achilles, he knows nothing of loyalty to the state or even to the cause for which he presumably fights. But in the age of the poet a new spirit, that of the Crusades, and a new concept of French unity and nationalism were in the ascendancy. The Crusades provided knighthood with a cause, and the Capetian kings furnished it with a set of political principles which transcended the older feudal values, however heroic those may have seemed in retrospect.

The *Song of Roland* holds the two sets of standards in equilibrium. Despite their disagreement and Oliver's denunciation of Roland, the two heroes die reconciled, and Charlemagne's rousing defeat of the Saracen host accomplishes both feudal revenge and national, indeed international, victory. Thierry bases his case against Ganelon on the concept of corporate responsibility, but he must settle it by the feudal rite of personal conflict. And Charlemagne's final reluctance to obey Gabriel's command to summon all his forces for yet another war emphasizes the priority of the duties of kingship over the rights and preferences of the individual.

Something more should be said here of the Christianity

of the poem. Although most critics have always held the
Song of Roland to be "Christian to its very bones,"[12] George
Fenwick Jones's careful analysis of the language of the
poem demonstrates conclusively that its ethos is essentially
pagan. True, the cause for which the French fight is Christianity, and their statements of purpose as well as their
religious rites connote a Christian frame of reference. But as
Jones says, those beliefs that are "basic to Christianity"—
"the tenets that humility is better than pride, that love is
better than hate, and that forgiveness is better than vengeance"[13]—not only do not appear in the poem but are
actively refuted by the brutal feudal standards which motivate the action. Like *Beowulf* and, as we shall see, the *Nibelungenlied* and the Norse sagas, the *Song of Roland* is
only superficially Christian; the pagan values of the older
legend retain their hold over the action and spirit of the
poem. As in *Beowulf*, one could in fact remove the Christian
references without materially affecting either tone or plot:

> There was no place in [Archbishop] Turpin's company for
> the meek or the poor in spirit, no place for the merciful
> or the peacemakers. The peacemaker Ganelon is the villain
> of the song; the warmonger Roland is its hero. God sends
> special angels for Roland's soul, but not for that of his
> more reasonable friend Oliver. For the heroes of the *SR*,
> being persecuted or reviled would only prove cowardice
> and weakness; and failure to achieve revenge would bring
> everlasting shame. They would have ostracized any man
> who turned his other cheek.[14]

The superficiality of the poem's Christianity may be ac-
counted for in several ways. First, the conversion of Gaul
in the time of Clovis was hasty and utilitarian; the arguments of the new religion were frankly based on a "material-
istic bartering of earthly wealth for heavenly reward."[15] Also,
the warlike state of Europe during feudal and Viking days
kept alive the martial character of the pagan ethos.

More important for our study of the poem, however, is
the fact that a Christian heroic poem is a contradiction in

terms. Almost by definition, the hero, whether or not one approves of his values and his conduct, is a pagan. He is motivated by the most un-Christian of virtues—pride in his prowess and the desire for earthly glory. Temperance, mercy, and forgiveness are never heroic, however admirable.

This is the reason, I believe, that *The Faerie Queene* fails to excite or move most readers at its level of action and that Blake and many subsequent readers felt Satan to be the hero of *Paradise Lost*. Holiness is not a knightly virtue—witness the carefully restricted use of Galahad in the Arthurian tradition—and in combat Redcross more resembles Zeal than Holiness. And however much one may rationalize the position of the Son as hero of *Paradise Lost,* it is the defiant Satan of the first books who most reflects the heroic temper.

A natural conclusion then would be that while Roland and Beowulf may attend mass and outwardly pay their respects to the Christian God, they must, in order to fulfill the demands of the heroic code, be pagan in both their spirit and their actions. The heroic poet of the Middle Ages, whether English or French or Scandinavian, could like Homer place in equilibrium the social values of the past and present, but he could only superimpose the externals of Christianity upon the heroic paganism of the past.

The *Song of Roland* is thus no simple battle hymn extolling the virtues of a bygone age. It is rather a stirring of the new France, and indeed of the new Europe, and if Roland is its hero, its final victories fall to Charlemagne. But, like the Homeric epics, it sees the present in terms of the past and weeps for what has gone even as it praises what remains and is to come.

It was in every way the perfect song for Taillefer to sing at Hastings.

CHAPTER FIVE

The Nibelungenlied

In discussing the *Song of Roland* I carefully avoided one avenue of investigation followed in the preceding chapters—the relation of mythical hero and historical king. For while the *Song of Roland* follows closely the pattern of the Homeric epics in its tight, meaningful structure, in its use of history as modified by oral tradition, and in its contrasting of heroic and corporate values, its hero, unlike Achilles, Odysseus, and Beowulf, is a creature of history rather than myth. We know at least that he existed, fought at Roncevaux, and so distinguished himself as to be singled out in dispatches.

I am hesitant, therefore, to attempt to superimpose this aspect of the heroic pattern, the tension between mythical and historical figures, upon the *Song of Roland*. True, the twelve peers may reflect an ancient myth pattern by their possible connection with the months of the lunar year; and Roland, like most mythic heroes, is not permitted to be killed in battle by a Saracen blade but dies as a result of his exertions in blowing the olifant. And he certainly conforms as well to the "myth" of Jungian archetypes—the "eternal creature of the dream." But there is no evidence at all for ascribing to him an origin in either religious myth or folklore.

The hero (or at least one of the heroes) of the *Nibelungenlied,* on the other hand, retains his origin in Germanic mythology even after the nearly eight hundred years that separate historical from dramatic time in the poem. Siegfried, despite his rather prosaic parentage and his twelfth-century courtliness and refinement, is in the *Nibelungenlied* still much the same godlike figure who in the early myths slew the dragon and pierced the wall of flame surrounding Brunhild's castle. There is, to be sure, some slight evidence for the existence of a historical Siegfried and Brunhild, based for the most part on onomastics and rough similarities to incidents in Gothic history, but their story from its very beginnings smacks strongly of mythic origins—particularly the incident of Brunhild's awakening, which seems to have its ultimate origin in myths of the sun god and the sleeping beauty.

Strangely enough, however, the important sources for the Siegfried story are Scandinavian rather than German, although the legend itself is probably of Low German origin. The story probably originated among the Franks and was carried by traders or raiders to Scandinavia, perhaps as early as the sixth century. It first appeared in written form in a number of lays contained in the so-called *Elder Edda,* a collection of verses put together in the thirteenth century; and because most of these poems date from the earlier period of Viking conquests they preserve early Germanic myths and themes. Luckily, the songs of the *Elder Edda,* which deal with scattered events in the life of Siegfried, can be supplemented by the account of the hero in the prose *Volsunga saga,* essentially a paraphrase of the *Elder Edda,* which contains enough detail to place the earlier lays in a narrative context. The *Thidreks saga,* a thirteenth-century Norwegian saga dealing with the life of Dietrich of Berne, the historical Theodoric the Great, contains a lengthy retelling of the Siegfried story and is chiefly important because it derives not only from the earlier Scandinavian versions of the legend but also, as the author himself tells us, from the stories of North German merchants.

These three documents, along with some abbreviated forms of the tale in the *Prose Edda* of Snorri Sturluson and in the *Nornagests saga* (which despite their brevity add a number of details to the longer accounts) and some scattered allusions to it in various late medieval songs and poems (including *Beowulf*), constitute our main sources for the Siegfried legend. Without attempting to recount these early forms of the legend in all their conflicting detail or to reduce them to an Ur-Siegfried, let us summarize them briefly. They deal with a hero of divine origin, being descended from Odin, who early in life with the help of a miraculous sword kills a dragon, wins an enormous treasure, and is rendered invulnerable, save for a small spot between the shoulder blades, by the dragon's blood. He goes on to rescue the sleeping Brunhild from a magic circle of fire and gives her a ring of betrothal, only to leave her after a short time to pursue his adventures. He arrives at the court of Guiki where under the influence of a potion he marries the king's daughter, Kriemhild.[1] Siegfried assists Gunther, one of Kriemhild's brothers, in wooing Brunhild by riding through the fire circle and, later, by deceitfully subduing her on Gunther's behalf by spending a night at her side during which he replaces her betrothal ring with one taken from the treasure.

In time Kriemhild and Brunhild become involved in a deadly wrangle concerning the relative nobility of their husbands, and Brunhild learns of Siegfried's deception. When Kriemhild shows her the fatal ring, Brunhild prevails upon Gunther's and Kriemhild's brother Hagen to arrange the death of Siegfried, using as a pretext an opportunity for Hagen to acquire the treasure. Siegfried is killed; Brunhild commits suicide; and Kriemhild after a period of several years marries Etzel, who murders her brothers to possess Siegfried's treasure and is in turn killed by her.

It should be clear from even so brief a summary that Siegfried and Brunhild are creatures of myth. Siegfried, as a matter of fact, scores eleven points out of a possible twenty-two on Lord Raglan's scale:

> His mother, Siglinde, is (1) a princess, and his father is (2) King Sigmund, who is (3) her brother, and whom she (4) visits in the guise of another woman. On reaching manhood he (10) performs a journey, (11) slays a dragon, (12) marries a princess, and (13) becomes a ruler. For a time he (14) prospers, but later (16) there is a plot

against him, and he is killed. He is (19) the only man who can pass through a ring of fire to a hilltop.[2]

One might add to this list the facts that Siegfried is descended from the gods; that he, like Achilles, is invulnerable from attack, save in one spot; and that he is able, having tasted the dragon's blood, to communicate with the birds. Brunhild in the older legends likewise shows mythic ancestry. There are various tests, passing through a ring of fire or taming a horse, which the hero must pass to marry her, and the *Thidreks saga* states that her great strength is dependent upon her virginity.

Both Siegfried and Brunhild, moreover, carry vestiges of their origins into the courtly world of the *Nibelungenlied* and so seem strangely ill at ease in the elegant court of Gunther and Kriemhild. Like Achilles, Siegfried is essentially an isolated figure, and though he assists Gunther to woo Brunhild, he does so for purely selfish reasons. And like Achilles, he is proud and arrogant beyond any requirement of the heroic code. Although he assures his father that he will conduct his courtship first by "friendly requests,"[3] and by force only if these fail, he in fact answers Gunther's courteous welcoming speech with the haughty demand that Gunther turn over to him all his land, castles, and people. (He does not, interestingly enough, even mention to Gunther at this meeting his desire to wed Kriemhild.) It takes all the diplomacy that Gunther and his advisers can muster to pacify the arrogant young lad.

Furthermore, the poet is careful to mention Siegfried's supernatural accomplishments when he is introduced into the action. When Siegfried approaches Gunther's castle, Hagen recognizes him and tells Gunther at some length of the hero's acquiring of the treasure (in this version, from two mighty princes, Schilbung and Nibelung, and an accompanying force of twelve giants and seven hundred warriors), his winning of the *Tarnkappe* which renders its wearer invisible, and his battle with the dragon.

In the days that follow, Siegfried is indeed somewhat tamed by the Burgundian court, "for he aspired to a noble love" (p. 31); yet when the opportunity arises to prove his valor in Gunther's war against the Saxons, his old arrogance returns, and having instructed Gunther to remain at home, he leads a force of one thousand Burgundians to victory against forty thousand Saxons.

Returning to Burgundy, he becomes again very much the courtier, but when he agrees to undertake Gunther's courtship of Brunhild, he spurns Gunther's offer of thirty thousand troops and will allow only Gunther, Hagen, and Dancwart to accompany him on the dangerous mission. In winning Brunhild for Gunther, he makes use not only of his almost supernatural strength but also of the *Tarnkappe;* he uses the magic cloak a second time in subduing Gunther's reluctant bride.

Siegfried's essential character is perhaps best revealed in his theft of Brunhild's ring and girdle. His motive must be sheer pride (as indeed the poet all but states directly), the kind of adolescent irresponsibility that underlies Achilles' sending Patroclus into battle and Roland's refusing to blow the olifant. In taking the ring and girdle and turning them over to Kriemhild, he obviously thinks himself immune to any sort of tragic consequences, and this attitude demonstrates clearly the arrogance that marks all his actions but those involved in his courtship of Kriemhild.

Even his last actions, save one, are marked by heroic arrogance. Upon being told that the Saxons are again threatening the Burgundians, he flies into an almost egomaniacal rage:

> I, Siegfried, shall prevent it with all energy, as befits your honour, and I will deal with them now as I dealt with them before. I shall lay waste their lands and castles before I have finished with them, let my head be your pledge for it! You and your warriors must stay at home and let me ride against them with the men that I have here. I shall show you how glad I am to help you. Believe me, I shall make your enemies suffer. (pp. 119–20)

And on his final hunt, having terrified the hunting party by loosing a captured bear in camp, he indulges in a fit of pique because no wine is brought to him: "Unless we hunters are better looked after," he says, "I'll not be a companion to the hunt. I thought I had deserved better attention" (p. 129).

Strangely enough, however, in describing Siegfried's murder the poet suggests that the hero's assumed courtliness rather than his inherent *hubris* is directly responsible for his death: on reaching the spring, Siegfried courteously stands aside to allow Hagen time to dispose of Siegfried's bow and sword; the poet then comments significantly that Siegfried "paid for his good manners" (p. 130).

Brunhild, though her role in the *Nibelungenlied* is much reduced from the early versions of the story, asserts her mythic origins in much the same way. She is clearly related to the fairytale figure of the sleeping beauty. She rules alone in splendid isolation in Isenland, there imposing a series of well-nigh impossible tasks on her suitors, failure in which carries a penalty of death. As in the older legends, she greets the initial wedding-night advances of Gunther with scorn and violence. She is perpetually concerned over Siegfried's apparent failure to pay his feudal obligations, and not only is she quick to challenge Kriemhild's suggestion that Gunther is not Siegfried's overlord but also, "enthroned in her pride," she refuses to mourn the death of Siegfried (p. 144).

As with Siegfried, however, the poet apparently has taken pains to subdue the barbarian spirit of the mythical Brunhild. There is no indication, for example, that she suggests to either Gunther or Hagen that Siegfried be murdered; and the poet has omitted, perhaps deliberately, her exultant laugh upon hearing of Siegfried's death. Most important is the fact that Brunhild does not commit suicide but simply disappears from the action of the poem.

But both Siegfried and Brunhild, though softened considerably by time and by the courtly interests of the poet, retain something of their mythic origins. To be sure, Siegfried is no longer the "youthful day who is destined to rouse the sun [Brunhild] from her slumber," nor is he the "bright summer" who has overthrown the dragon of winter and the dwarfs of darkness,[4] but the poet does retain enough of the hero's original character and exploits to separate him rather sharply from those "new men" with whom he has come to dwell, particularly Gunther and Hagen.

Gunther, and presumably the members of his court as well, are, like Agamemnon and Hygelac, ultimately descendants from history rather than from myth and, as in the Homeric epics and *Beowulf*, their origins have considerable bearing upon their roles in the poem. The *Lex Burgundionum*, a sixth-century chronicle, mentions among a list of earlier rulers of Burgundy one Gundaharius, almost certainly the Gunther of the poem, who established the Burgundian nation along the Rhine in the first years of the fifth century. In 435 the Burgundians revolted against their Roman overlords and were defeated by the Roman general Aetius. They rebelled again, however, the following year and this time were almost annihilated by a combination of Roman and Hunnish forces. Attila apparently did not himself take part in this engagement—most certainly he did not die in it—in which some twenty thousand Burgundians were killed, but it is quite natural that he, the archetype of the voracious Hun, later became associated with the slaughter.

The tenth-century Latin epic *Waltharius*, devoted to the exploits of Walter of Aquitaine, mentions a few of the *Nibelungenlied* characters, though it does not relate them to the slaughter of the Burgundians. Two of the lays of the *Elder Edda* deal with Etzel's marriage to Gunther's sister and his consequent destruction of the Burgundians in an attempt to gain the Nibelung treasure: the *Atla Kvidha*, dating back to the ninth century, and the *Brot*, a fragment of an Eddic lay on the death of Siegfried. There is no hint in either lay, however, of the role of avenger later assumed by Kriemhild; in the *Elder Edda* Etzel is the sole villain and his motive is the theft of the treasure.

Thidreks saga not only connects the Siegfried story with that of the Burgundians' destruction through the motif of Kriemhild's revenge but also introduces into the action Dietrich of Berne. Dietrich is the historical Theodoric the Great who, although he is in the poem living in exile at Etzel's court, actually died in 526, almost a hundred years after the dramatic period of the action. Significantly, in the *Thidreks saga* Etzel is no longer the instigator of the slaughter but has become Kriemhild's tool in her revenge.

While it is impossible here to untangle the complex web of sources, a few generalizations are possible. First, there is no clear source for the *Nibelungenlied,* although scholars have freely manufactured hypothetical ancestors, particularly the so-called *Diu Nôt* of 1160.[5] Second, the poem has its ultimate origin in two kinds of material: a myth involving a dragon-killer and the maiden whom he rescues, and the historical destruction of the Burgundians by the Huns. Third, while the exact cause and circumstances of the union of myth and history are of course unknown,[6] a statement of Saxo Grammaticus in 1131 referring to "Kriemhild's famous betrayal of her brothers" demonstrates that the change necessary to that union—Kriemhild's revenge—had been accomplished at least by that date.

The poem as we have it thus stands at the end of a long period of development for which we have very few documents. Nor do we have any evidence of the existence of an oral tradition, though it seems to me safe to assume that one existed since, despite this paucity of sources, the development of the complex story of the fall of the Nibelungs can be seen to be marked by the same sort of changes we have noted elsewhere. There is the same combination of mythical and historical elements and the same distortion of history. And I think it demonstrable also that the poem exhibits the blending of past and present standards of conduct and the fusion of heroic and corporate values that so mark the heroic as a type.

But with a startling difference. Unlike the Homeric epics, *Beowulf,* and the *Song of Roland,* the *Nibelungenlied* was not written at a time in which a new, highly organized, nationalistic civilization was beginning to emerge from a long period of political chaos and confusion. Quite the opposite, in fact. Germany had suffered less than any other western kingdom from the collapse of the post-Carolingian kingdoms in the late ninth century and thus was able not only to preserve some semblance of order in the centuries that followed but also, through its almost universal military conscription, to beat off the Viking attacks which were paralyzing the rest of western Europe. Moreover, the strong rule of Otto I in the late ninth century prevented, or at least delayed, the rise of feudalism in Germany. In fact, had it not been for the continuing quarrels between the German emperors and the eleventh- and twelfth-century popes, Germany might have avoided completely the feudal disunity that plagued the emerging nations of medieval Europe.

But by the mid-twelfth century the German emperors had largely lost control of their empire. They might still jockey for power in the never-ending game of playing baron against bishop, but they had little or no authority of their own. Even the greatest of the Hohenstaufens, Frederick Barbarossa, was unable to bring together in his forty-one-year reign the remnants of the Ottonian Empire, Germany and northern Italy; despite his astute political maneuvering, he was forced to overextend what were at best limited powers and so succeeded neither in uniting a Germany torn by the feud of Guelphs and Ghibellines nor in annexing an Italy united under papal auspices against him. And with the death of Frederick's heir, Henry VI, in 1197, Frederick's advances toward unity quickly disintegrated in a maelstrom of renewed civil wars. From the time of the writing of the *Nibelungenlied* until the end of the Middle Ages, there was no effective central government in the Ottonian Empire: in Italy each city-state governed its own affairs; in Germany the individual principalities remained autonomous.

Despite the barbarism of the times, however, the Viennese court, which the poet, whatever his status, doubtless knew well, considered itself a haven of culture and refinement. Declared a *civitas* in 1137, Vienna under the Babenbergs had become a provincial center of both commerce and art. Yet this culture, largely imported from France, had no real relation to its setting, existing as it did in the midst of political turmoil which might at any minute destroy it and upon which it had no visible influence. The reign of the Ghibelline Philip of Swabia, during which the *Nibelungenlied* was written, was as precarious as it was brief. His election as emperor was immediately challenged by the Guelphs, who with the support of the pope placed against him Otto of Brunswick. The renewed feud over the imperial crown between the princes of Church and State raged in such fury that Philip could not be crowned until 1205 and was assassinated in 1208. The new ideals of chivalry might well exist in the courtly romances imported from France and imitated by German poets; Emperor Philip and the margraves of Babenberg might even try to create for themselves an atmosphere of sophisticated courtliness. But the realities of German politics demanded that the nation's great lords adopt ruthless and calculated policies far removed from the chivalric values of the more settled French courts of the period.

It has often been remarked that the *Nibelungenlied* presents a startling contrast of courtly and barbaric conduct, and it is hardly surprising that this should be true. The poet certainly had occasion to observe the gulf between the imported, largely artificial standards of chivalry and the harsh, practical laws of political survival. *Gentilesse*, whatever its virtues and graces, perished or was at best simply pushed aside in the apparently never-ending struggle for power between Guelph and Ghibelline. A Siegfried softened by the amenities of court life became the easy prey of an unscrupulous Hagen, and a naive Etzel the tool of an unprincipled Kriemhild.

The legend of Siegfried and the fall of the Nibelungs emerged, as we have said, as the *Nibelungenlied* after a very long period of germination. In its seeds doubtless lay all sorts of possibilities for development and interpretation. But the form it finally took in the one finished poem that has survived is almost certainly attributable to the perception and genius of the man who composed it. Unlike Homer, he could not look back from a newly emerged and already settled commercial state across the gulf of a dark age to a more individualistic, albeit more barbarous, age of heroes.

Had he known Greek history, he might well have imagined himself instead to be still inhabiting the dark chaos of post-Mycenaean times, looking back through the confused tales of heroic legend to an even less settled, though ostensibly more heroic, time but forward only to the uncertain conflict of warlords. Still the legend itself, even if it did not offer a solution, might at least provide the poet with a means of defining the times. For it might be shaped into an image of the debilitation of the heroic Ottonian code into ineffectual *luxuria* on the one hand and unprincipled barbarism on the other.

The *Nibelungenlied* is thus a poem without a single hero. To a degree far greater than had Homer, the poet makes of the old legend a contemporary poem, and he finds no real heroes in his own time. Without ever descending to the level of political allegory, the reshaped legend defines the central issues of early thirteenth-century Germany: the barbarous, self-destructive warfare between states, the ineffectual leadership of the rulers, the seizure of power by the ruthless and the treacherous, the lack of concern for national welfare, the failure of the Church to maintain order, and the more universal failure of the nobility to live by the chivalric code which it professed or indeed by any standard of decent behavior.

And these themes are everywhere supported by the poem's tone of despair, by its sense of futility, and by its sure knowledge that joy must end in sorrow—not, as in *Beowulf* and the Norse sagas, because the gods themselves cannot prevent it but because man in his perversity so wills it. From beginning to end, from Kriemhild's dream to Dietrich's and Etzel's laments, the poet foretells the dreadful consequences of unprincipled action. He is careful to frame the story with a clear statement of its theme: the young Kriemhild tries to avoid marriage because "there are many examples of women who have paid for happiness with sorrow in the end," and after the final slaughter we are again reminded that "joy must ever turn to sorrow in the end" (pp. 18, 291).

But the structure of the poem provides the most convenient point of departure for a discussion of its general intent and its relation to the heroic tradition. The bipartite form of the legend—the crude joining of the stories of Siegfried's death and the Burgundians' destruction by the single strand of Kriemhild's revenge—was at once the poet's greatest problem and the means by which he could best present his theme. There can be no doubt that the coupling of myth and history presented enormous difficulties of structure. The extended chronology and complex relations of the major characters made the *in medias res* technique of the *Odyssey* impossible; one simply could not summarize by retrospective narrative the complicated events of Adventures 1–9, nor was there a single character who could be made to report them with any degree of objectivity. The "natural" way of treating the story, on the other hand, straight chronological narration, could easily, because of its premature first climax (the death of Siegfried) and its tendency to degenerate into a series of personal combats, blunt or even completely obscure the theme which the poet wished at all costs to express.

His answer to this technical problem was to adopt a chronology which, though linear and straightforward, varies in tempo and intensity according to his needs, moving from a deceptively leisurely beginning to a swiftly moving climax and conclusion. The exposition is handled slowly and carefully, allowing the reader to fix in mind clearly the essential qualities of the characters, particularly Kriemhild's pride and Siegfried's rash haughtiness. With the arrival of Siegfried at Worms, Kriemhild is temporarily put aside in order to introduce Gunther and Hagen and to develop, through the apparently digressive Saxon war, Siegfried's prowess. Only then does the poet permit Siegfried to see Kriemhild and introduce the first stirrings of romance. Next he introduces Brunhild through Gunther's journey to Isenland, and the contrast between Siegfried and Gunther is reinforced through Siegfried's conduct in the games and his journey to the hall of the Nibelungs. With Siegfried's return the poet turns to the romance of Siegfried and Kriemhild and relates Siegfried's subduing of the prideful Brunhild.

Up to this point he has proceeded in leisurely fashion, relating the principal events, the journeys and trials, in the unhurried spirit of the French romance. And indeed, were it not for the absence of the endless psychologizing of Chrétien's heroes and heroines, the reader would almost imagine himself to be reading an *Yvain* or an *Erec and Enide*. The tone is courtly and elegant save for an occasional outburst by Siegfried, and the formalities of court life are described in detail; were it not for the foreshadowings of the dark days to come, one would be deceived into expecting a happy issue from the events. Yet the apparently discursive nature of the narrative is not without its effect, for it plants securely in incident after incident the seeds of later action: the fierce Siegfried is lulled into a false security by the sophisticated manners of an alien court; Kriemhild's youthful independence is overmatched by her growing love for Siegfried; Hagen's devotion to his lord, Gunther, is everywhere apparent. The gay atmosphere of the Burgundian court is, like the courtly tone of the poem, a willful deception.

This tone is broken sharply at Adventure 14, "How the Queens Railed at Each Other," and the suspense of the narrative is increased, event following event more swiftly now and almost without elaboration. With the argument of Kriemhild and Brunhild the niceties of court life are abandoned, and the participants begin to reveal their essential characters. Siegfried treats the affair with cavalier self-confidence; Gunther avoids the issue by hedging;[7] Kriemhild, though dutifully submitting to her husband's judgment and a beating, is apprehensive and fears for his life; and Hagen, inflamed at the insult to Gunther's wife, weaves a complex web of deceit to redress the wrong. The courtly tone returns briefly in the elaborate hunt which follows, but it serves only to increase suspense and to set the stage for Hagen's brutal murder of Siegfried.

From the death of Siegfried until the arrival of the Burgundians in Hungary the tempo of action slows down again, though the prevailing tone is sorrow rather than the festival joy of the early books. Kriemhild's alternating grief and rage, even in the midst of her marriage festivities, are dwelt upon by the poet in preparation for her new role in the days to come, and indeed all the characters reveal themselves more and more during this interval: Gunther becomes more irresolute, Hagen firmer and grimmer. The journey to Hungary itself is enormously expanded by the poet. As the Burgundians pass milestone after milestone—the warnings by Hagen, the incidents of the rude ferryman and the fated chaplain, the attack by Gelpfrat, even the idyllic stay at Pöchlarn—they are met by portents of the terror to come. Every incident, even Rudiger's innocent gift of a sword to Gernot, is wreathed round by ironies indicating that the Burgundians will never retrace their steps to their homeland.

With the arrival of Gunther's army at Etzel's court in Hungary, the poet abandons the joyful courtliness of the first books, the mounting suspense of the days preceding Siegfried's murder, and the steadily darkening mood of the middle books to break forth into a strident narrative that fairly leaps from crisis to crisis and battle to battle. The great tableaux follow each other in breathless succession: Hagen refusing to arise at Kriemhild's approach, Kriemhild begging Dietrich for escort through the slaughter of the banquet hall, Volker fiddling the battle-weary Burgundians to sleep, Hagen restoring Rudiger's honor by begging from him his shield. No room now for courtliness or suspense or sorrow; everything is subordinated to the swift pace of the action, and when at last the climax comes and Kriemhild at the height of her savagery executes Hagen with Siegfried's sword, the tale is done. No funeral games or denouement as in Homer, no funeral lament as in *Beowulf,* no commission to continue the struggle as in the *Song of Roland* remain to be recounted. The poem ends upon a shrieking discord of destruction, its final note, like its first, a grim reminder that "joy must ever turn to sorrow in the end."

The poet thus solves the chronological problem of his highly discursive material by alternating both tone and tempo according to his immediate needs, principally those of characterization and mood. But even more important than the problem of chronology was the difficulty of producing the necessary change in the character of Kriemhild, who must be transformed from a sympathetic heroine and widow to a vicious monster whose death we welcome. In the hands of the *Nibelungenlied*-poet this apparent obstacle to a unified structure becomes itself a means of unification; whatever its sources may have been, the *Nibelungenlied* as we have it is Kriemhild's poem. She is the first character to appear and her death is the last event. There is hardly an action in the entire poem which she does not in some way motivate or in which she is not directly involved. Hagen, grim and terrible as he is, and Gunther, the only other major characters who bridge the gap between the two halves of the poem, seldom take upon themselves the responsibility of action; whatever greatness they finally achieve lies in their resistance to the overwhelming force of her character.

The poet's greatest accomplishment in characterization, and through characterization, in unity, is that he is able to develop the character of Kriemhild from obstinate maiden to charming bride to grief-stricken widow to revengeful devil convincingly and meaningfully. And this is no mean accomplishment for the medieval poet, who tended either to think of characters simply as "the people who did those deeds"[8] or to envisage them as acting, as do Roland and the Norse heroes, from fixed traits of character. The notion that a character can be "round," to use E. M. Forster's happy term, and hence apparently contradictory is a late development in fiction. And though certainly Kriemhild is no round character, yet her development in the poem is as carefully planned as that of a Jamesian heroine.

We first see her as a charming, though willful, girl, yet the poet assures us that she is fated to cause the deaths of many knights. This ominous foreshadowing, one of the poet's most notable traits, not only immediately prefigures the dark days to come but also places the blame for the tragedy upon Kriemhild—specifically upon the "enmity of two noble ladies" and the "terrible vengeance she took on her nearest kinsman" (pp. 17, 19). There can be little doubt that the poet is fully aware of the changes that future events are to make in the character of Kriemhild and that he is here preparing us for these changes.

Kriemhild's own reaction to her dream of the ill-fated falcon destroyed by two eagles clearly establishes the strain of fierce pride and independence that is later to dominate her whole character. She vows to her mother that she will never marry since she intends to keep her beauty until death and "never be made wretched by the love of any man" (p. 18). She knows of many women who "have paid for happiness with sorrow in the end," and by not marrying she hopes to "avoid both." But she has not yet met Siegfried.

Though Kriemhild disappears from the action during Siegfried's arrival at the Burgundian court, his war with the Saxons, and his courtship of Brunhild on behalf of Gunther, her presence is constantly felt. It is to win her that Siegfried performs his great deeds, and we are gradually made aware of her growing affection for him. We are told how she watches him from her window as he takes part in the games and how she regrets his absence when he rides on circuit with the other knights. She blushes with relief when he returns from the Saxon campaign, and at their first meeting she takes his hand and the two exchange tender looks in secret. When the time finally comes for her betrothal, she has fallen so in love with Siegfried that, her statements to her mother forgotten, she grants without demur her brother's request that she marry the young lord.

Her pride having been conquered by love, she becomes in every way the devoted, dutiful wife. Yet we are not allowed by the poet to forget the strength of her character. At Siegfried's announcement that they are to go to his home in the Netherlands, she states that she must first receive from her brothers her proper share of her family's lands. Siegfried pridefully overrules her and rejects Gunther's offer of the property. However, while accepting without comment Siegfried's renunciation of her inheritance, she nevertheless insists that proper honor and allegiance be shown to her, demanding that one-third of the household knights form her retinue. Her interest here in preserving her own property and the allegiance due her does much to explain her later indignation over Hagen's theft of Siegfried's treasure.

It has often been remarked that Kriemhild is responsible for the quarrel between the two queens that precipitates the murder of Siegfried. Yet such is not strictly the case. True, Kriemhild's remark upon watching Siegfried in the games that she has "a husband of such merit that he might rule over all the kingdoms of this region" actually invokes the argument (p. 111), but it is from her point of view a simple expression of joy in her husband's prowess. Brunhild, however, has brooded for over ten years on the apparent failure of Siegfried to render his proper feudal obligations to Gunther and so willfully interprets Kriemhild's casual remark as a slight to her own and, she believes, higher-born husband. But Kriemhild in all innocence goes on praising Siegfried until Brunhild's blunt statement that Siegfried is Gunther's vassal brings her up short. Immediately, her fierce pride aroused, she retaliates by daring to enter the church before Brunhild, who as reigning queen could rightfully assume the privilege of entering first. Furthermore, her anger now having completely usurped her judgment, she reveals the dreaded secret of Brunhild's wedding night and produces the ring and girdle which Siegfried in his boyish pride had taken. Siegfried and Gunther are able to calm the waters, even to the extent of punishing their wives, but Kriemhild's pride has sealed both their fates.

Yet Kriemhild has not yet become the terrifying character who will murder Hagen. Her revelation of Siegfried's vulnerability is, like her statements of pride in his prowess, an act of innocence, this time motivated by a genuine concern for her husband's welfare; weeping, she begs him not to attend the fatal hunt. Upon receiving the news of his death, she faints, but upon awakening, in one shriek she commits her whole life to revenge. "If I knew who had done this," she cries, "I should never cease to plot his death" (p. 134).

There is little need to describe in detail Kriemhild's actions in the final section of the poem except perhaps at a few critical points. For no matter how strange and contradictory her individual acts may seem, they are actually all of a piece; they all come from her pride, transformed by the death of Siegfried, who alone could subdue it, into a passion for revenge which never for an instant leaves her mind. First, she refuses to return to the Netherlands with Siegmund. This is, on the surface at least, a strange decision, for she not only remains in the midst of her husband's murderers but also renounces her rightful role as queen and, more important, as mother. She then suddenly becomes concerned with the disposition of Siegfried's treasure, her nuptial dowry, and is furious when Hagen steals it. Next she marries Etzel, a stranger and a pagan. Finally, she apparently sacrifices Ortlieb, her son by Etzel, in what seems to be a meaningless act of brutality.

Yet all these actions, contradictory and motiveless if taken one by one, are parts of a carefully wrought pattern of character development. The vow of revenge which Kriemhild takes upon Siegfried's death underlies her every subsequent action, and the two apparently irreconcilable strands of her character so carefully established in the first part of the poem, her fierce natural pride and her adoration of her husband, are in one awful moment turned into a single unbreakable cord of anger and passion. For revenge she will forsake throne and child and so, like Lady Macbeth, deliberately unsex herself; she will fight for her treasure, not for itself but only for its power to support her in her cause. For revenge she will marry a heathen; for revenge she will sacrifice her child to enlist the aid of Etzel.[9] One by one the great heroes and allies of the Hungarians yield to her passion. No means, no device, no trick is beneath her; every decent impulse, every scruple must be suppressed. Bribery, cajolery, threats are her weapons; that Dietrich must sacrifice his men and Rudiger his soul in order that she accomplish her ends is of no consequence to her. It is altogether fitting, and consistent, that at the end she should execute Hagen with Siegfried's sword. The charming maiden who once blushed at the name of Siegfried must personally even the score.

I have dwelt at some length on the role of Kriemhild to demonstrate that the poet has used the startling change in her character which he inherited from the Nibelung tradition as a means of unifying the poem. But this analysis should also show that Kriemhild in becoming the structural center of the poem becomes also its thematic center: whatever values and attitudes the poet professes are expressed in her character and actions. And the key to her character and actions can be plainly seen in the utterly unscrupulous barbarism of her campaign for revenge. Her willful and prideful nature is conquered briefly by love, but, roused by the murder of her husband, reasserts itself with such force that it destroys two powerful nations. In accomplishing her revenge, moreover, Kriemhild steps completely outside the normal bounds of decent human conduct; she conducts herself according to no acknowledged standards of civilized behavior. Loyalty, truthfulness, understanding, consideration for others, mercy—these mean nothing to her.

Integrity, if the word be interpreted to mean a single-minded devotion to one's cause, however self-centered, she may be said to have; and it is her undoubtable integrity that has led some critics to see in her something of the indomitable, individualistic spirit of the epic hero. But hers is an integrity and an individualism run wild. Like Achilles sulking in his tent, Beowulf attacking the firedrake single-handed, and Roland refusing to summon help, Kriemhild is obsessed by a *hubris* that blinds her to the consequences of her actions. But unlike Achilles, Beowulf, and Roland, she never for a moment perceives her folly. Achilles is at last brought to reality by Priam and Roland by the sight of his slaughtered army, but Kriemhild dies unshaken by the devastation she has caused. She thus represents the furthest extension of one facet of the heroic temper: obsessed and proud, the hero becomes a monster.

Kriemhild's counterpart among the Burgundians is, of course, Hagen, and he is in every way her equal, though his heroic barbarism stems from a motive different from hers. If Kriemhild's *hubris* results from an exaggerated sense of integrity, then Hagen's character emerges from the opposing chivalric virtue, loyalty to one's master and concern for his welfare. Just as Kriemhild is willing to sacrifice her brothers, her husband, her child, and her nation to avenge a personal wrong, so Hagen is willing to plot, murder, and sacrifice his nation to protect Gunther. Siegfried is warned by his father of Hagen before he sets forth to woo Kriemhild, and it is only at Gernot's command that Hagen refrains from answering Siegfried's peremptory challenge when the young hero arrives at Worms. It is Hagen who suggests that Siegfried fight the Saxons since Gunther cannot assemble his forces in time and Hagen who proposes that Siegfried assist Gunther in the courtship of Brunhild. During their stay in Isenland Hagen time and again expresses his fear that Gunther will fail in the brutal games which Brunhild proposes. At Kriemhild's suggestion that he become her vassal, Hagen becomes furious and vows that he will follow no master but Gunther.

His loyalty to Gunther is his only motive in murdering Siegfried, but for Hagen it is motive enough. Coming upon Brunhild in tears, he immediately vows that Siegfried will suffer for having offended Gunther's queen. Gunther, true to his placid nature, is inclined to overlook the quarrel, but Hagen—like Kriemhild, dedicated forever to a vow taken in an instant—plies his master's feeble, though greedy, will with hopes of acquiring Siegfried's lands. Nor will he leave off his urging until master yields to vassal and he is permitted to arrange the complex deception by which he is able to elicit from Kriemhild the secret of Siegfried's vulnerable spot and so treacherously destroy the young hero.

But like integrity in Kriemhild, fidelity in Hagen breeds barbarity rather than heroic valor. Just as there is no real need for Kriemhild to sacrifice her child, so there is no excuse for Hagen's placing Siegfried's body outside Kriemhild's door. Yet again, as in Kriemhild, *hubris* in Hagen does not obscure intelligence or political cunning, both of which he devotes singlemindedly to the fulfillment of his vow. He gains control of Siegfried's treasure and later destroys it, not from greed but because he realizes that Kriemhild would buy supporters with it. He urges Gunther against the ill-fated journey to Hungary, not from cowardice but because he alone realizes the depth of Kriemhild's hatred. On arriving in Hungary he advises Gunther to heed Dietrich's warnings. However, once taunted by Gernot's assaults on his loyalty and honor, once assured by his failure to kill the chaplain (prophesied to be the only survivor of the expedition) that destruction is inevitable, Hagen becomes in effect the leader of the Burgundians—indomitable, fearless, and, like Kriemhild, utterly committed to his vow to protect Gunther.

If in his last days of stubborn resistance he reaches a kind of grandeur, it is a grandeur born of desperation, and, like Satan's in the early books of *Paradise Lost,* it is the grandeur of the prideful damned. Loyalty has bred guile, guile murder, and murder a cold, haughty cruelty. Yet Hagen is given one great moment, as Kriemhild is not. Recognizing the plight of the innocent, haunted, noble Rudiger, Hagen allows him to save face, to become again the patron rather than the victim of the Burgundians by begging from him his shield and repaying him with immunity from his own dread blows, an exchange which "good Rudiger acknowledged . . . with a polite bow" (p. 272). Even so, the incident seems to have been included to complete the poet's treatment of Rudiger rather than to soften our judgment of Hagen. It is fitting that in his last breath Hagen refuses to yield to Kriemhild the secret of Siegfried's treasure even though she promises his life in return (a promise she doubtless had no intention of keeping).

If Kriemhild and Hagen represent the ideals of chivalry, integrity, and loyalty reduced to barbarous cruelty, Gunther represents another possibility of failure in the chivalric code— its lapse into courtly vanity and ineffectualness. He relies on Hagen for every decision and can be maneuvered even into participating in murder at Hagen's urging. He is completely shaken and confused by Siegfried's first challenge and is all too willing, again at Hagen's urging, to allow the young stranger to fight his wars and even to do his courting. His habitual deceit and treachery are shown clearly in his allowing Siegfried to subdue his bride and later in publicly glossing over Siegfried's part in the affair. Although he plainly connives in the murder of Siegfried, and for the basest possible motive, he washes his hands of the matter by denying his complicity. Here he is plainly contrasted with Hagen, who comes to glory in his murder of Siegfried, treacherous as it is, as a symbol of his supreme loyalty to his master. True, at the end Gunther gains in stature by his conduct in battle, but only after he has tried and failed to lay the entire blame for the first battle on the Hungarians' massacre of the squires and has exhausted the possibilities of reconciliation.

Gunther, then, represents a chivalry gone to seed. He is at home only in the peaceful dalliance of his own court, contentedly enjoying the mock battles and petty intrigues of princely life. The difficult tasks of warfare and courtship he is willing to leave to others, and when a time finally comes in which glibness and deceit will no longer serve, he placidly allows Hagen to lead him into destruction.

The minor figures exhibit in much the same way the failure of thirteenth-century German chivalry to provide a fully operative standard of behavior. Etzel is naive and ineffectual to the point of foolishness, and Gernot and Giselher seem the pawns of their elder brother. Only Rudiger stands out, and it may well be that the poet is using him as an index of the fate of good men in troubled times. Indeed, had he survived, Rudiger might well have emerged as the hero of the poem. Kind, generous, brave, loyal, he is a paragon of chivalric virtue. His court is happy and free from the intrigues that plague Gunther's palace. Yet he is destroyed by the times, and the instrument of his destruction is his own good conscience. In making every possible effort to fulfill Etzel's commission to court Kriemhild on the king's behalf— and he is the best possible choice for the mission—Rudiger swears a personal oath of loyalty to Kriemhild, an oath closely related to his feudal oath to Etzel. Surely no harm could come from such a well-meaning gesture. Later he entertains the Burgundians lavishly on their way to Hungary and, again in good faith, acts as their escort. He even pledges his daughter's hand to the young Giselher. When the conflict comes he is thus caught between two sets of values, his feudal oaths and his natural duties to his guests and family. Although critics have maintained that he overstates his case,[10] he nevertheless believes that he has perjured his soul, that either choice will be disastrous both on earth and in Heaven. Significantly, he expresses here the only Christian doctrine contained in the poem.

Nor will Kriemhild release Rudiger from his terrible dilemma even though he offers to return his fiefs. Both she and Etzel beg and plead and wheedle until Rudiger, at last exhausted by their entreaties, relents and goes brokenhearted into battle. It is, as we have said, Hagen who releases him by allowing him to assert his chivalric manhood and to display in a single greathearted gesture his essential nobility. In the end Rudiger dies, ironically the victim of the very sword he had given Gernot during the happy days at Pöchlarn.

In the death of Rudiger one senses the fate of all good Christian men and the ultimate failure of chivalry in the war-torn Germany of the poet's age. In a world ruled by the weak and the treacherous and dominated by the ruthless, true lordship, true integrity, true loyalty (and surely Rudiger represents all three) are caught up in a whirlpool of conflicting values and are destroyed by their own perversions.

The *Nibelungenlied* is, in the end, a testament of despair. The poet may indeed have been able to look back to the myths and events of the distant past, to the very origins of the traditions he inherited—the springtime, magical world of a matchless Siegfried and a shining Brunhild, the heroic figure of a Kriemhild defending her brothers against the treachery of her barbarian husband, and the organized empire of Otto I—but the poem shows no evidence of such a vista. For in the course of time and history Siegfried had become merely boyish, Brunhild merely jealous, and the loyal sister a harridan. It remained for the poet to record forever the degeneration of the bright dream of heroism.

CHAPTER SIX

The Icelandic Sagas

The *Nibelungenlied* reveals one more variation of the heroic theme in that it fully exploits the mood of total despair apparent only as a contingency in the other poems we have examined. It is thus most like *Beowulf* and least like the *Odyssey,* though the thread of disillusionment with the heroic code runs through all heroic poetry. For the heroic poet is, above everything else, a strong realist even though he works with the materials of romance. As we have seen, he is an inheritor of the past, and as he looks back along the mazes of myth and history, he comprehends the values of past and present simultaneously but is committed to neither.

This is perhaps another reason that the writing of heroic poetry is denied the Christian poet, who is after all deeply committed not only to a Christian ethos but also to an optimistic theory of history in which the City of Man moves at the will of God toward the City of God and in which human progress is not only possible but also inevitable. From this metaphor and this theory of history the Christian writer may weave a hundred stories—the journey of a single man from the City of Destruction to the Heavenly City or of a whole society from London to Canterbury; but he can never rest content in the equilibrium of values—past balancing present, heroic balancing corporate—possible to the uncommitted pagan. By virtue of his religion he is denied the "negative capability" which Keats considered the hallmark of the greatest writers, the ability to remain in "uncertainties, mysteries, doubts, without any irritable reaching after facts and reason."[1] Thus Shakespeare, of whom Keats is speaking, never commits himself to any doctrine, even in *King Lear,* the most "religious" of the plays; while Chaucer, surely next to Shakespeare the most classically objective of all English authors, must in the end deny his uncommitted probings into the mysteries of Fortune in order to affirm his Christianity.

Thus, although Homer recognizes the presence of a cosmic order that is both stable and just, he is not committed, as is the Christian writer, to a particular view of man, nature, and history predetermined by particular religious doctrines—in the case of Christianity, the separation of God and man by a fall from grace and the redemption of man from this fallen state by an incarnate God—or by particular standards of conduct imposed by religion, for example, Christian forgiveness and humility. Homer is largely free within his cosmology to form his own view of the nature of man, society, and even of the gods. While the gods may occasionally interfere with the actions of the Greeks and the Trojans, they never determine the particular policies or characters or fates of the heroes, although these heroes are in the end subject to the immutable and universal laws of retribution and justice. Achilles is solely responsible for his own actions, however they may please or displease the gods, and Athene is not responsible for Odysseus's cunning, though she is attracted to him because of his intelligence.

The same is true even in the ostensibly Christian epics of the Middle Ages. The central events in the careers of Beowulf and Roland are in no way determined by their professed Christianity but rather by their deeply ingrained sense of heroic values. And aside from Rudiger's momentary fear for his soul—a dilemma that is finally resolved in heroic rather than Christian terms—there is nothing Christian, indeed nothing religious, in the *Nibelungenlied.* The *Nibelungenlied* is concerned solely with the nature of man and of a society utterly divorced from any theology or cosmology. The *Iliad* and the *Odyssey* place man against a just and ordered, and *Beowulf* a pessimistic, universe, but the *Nibelungenlied* sets man in isolation from the gods.

The Norse sagas, which also make little to-do over religion, are best understood against the backdrop of Scandinavian pessimism. Although Iceland was Christianized in the year 1000, its conversion had little, if any, effect upon the values of the sagas, whose heroes, like those of *Beowulf* and the *Nibelungenlied*, seem largely unaffected by Christian doctrines of charity and forbearance.[2] Fatalism, the belief that all events are predetermined by an immutable destiny, is fundamental to Nordic paganism. Snorri Sturluson, to whose *Prose Edda* we owe most of our knowledge of Scandinavian myth, states that "there is a beautiful hall near the spring under the ash tree [*Ygradasil*, which supports the universe], and from it come three maidens whose names are Urð, Verðandi, Skuld [past, present, future]. These maidens shape the lives of men, and we call them Norns." Snorri goes on to describe other Norns: good ones "from good stock shape good lives, but those who meet with misfortune owe it to the evil Norns."[3]

The events of a man's life are thus determined before his birth, and he is powerless to change them. Moreover, as we have seen in *Beowulf*, man's life is essentially tragic. He is doomed in advance to an unhappy fate which he is powerless to change in any way. He may, it is true, control his attitude toward his destiny: he may succumb to it, sniveling and cringing, or he may meet it head-on, heroically defying it. But the powers of fate cannot be averted nor can they be appeased.

Perhaps the best indication of this attitude, and hence of the essential difference between the prevailing mood of the Norse sagas and that of the *Nibelungenlied*, is to be found in the foreshadowing statements which fill both the sagas and the German epic. Generally speaking, these take three forms in the sagas: dreams, allusions to fate and destiny, and references to the good and bad luck of the characters.

Dreams appear frequently and are always used to presage tragic events. For example, Gudrun in *Laxdœla saga* has four dreams which forecast accurately the outcome of her four marriages; and at the very outset of *Gunnlaugs saga* Thorstein's dream of the contest between two eagles for a female swan foretells the strife between Gunnlaug and Hrafn for the hand of Helga. Even more impressive, Gisli in *Gisla saga* is haunted by a series of dreams in which an evil and a good woman advise him of his approaching fate. Indeed, in almost every saga dreams are used both structurally, to provide unity through the linking of present and future events, and thematically, to emphasize the inescapable destiny which awaits the hero.

The sagas are filled also with allusions to fate and destiny. Njal, the hero of *Njals saga,* is prescient and from the beginning knows his own destiny as well as those of other characters, as does Gest in *Laxdœla saga.* Gisli in *Gisla saga* continually refers to the impossibility of avoiding one's fate; Thorhall in *Thidrandi thattir* asserts that what is fated must happen; Thorstein in *Gunnlaugs saga* states that events are resolved as they are destined to be resolved; Asdis in *Grettis saga* prophesies the deaths of Illugi and Grettir on the island of Drangey and remarks that no man can escape his destiny. Indeed, it would be difficult to find a saga in which the narrative does not demonstrate the control of fate over the lives of men.

The presence of fate is often suggested by allusions to the good or bad luck which dominates a character's career and from which he cannot escape. Thus Grettir from the time of his battle with the supernatural Glam is haunted by misfortune. Thorir in *Hen-Thorir saga,* Sam in *Hrafnkels saga,* and Gisli in *Gisla saga* are said to be unlucky and hence are avoided by others; while Kjartan in *Laxdœla saga,* despite his fate, comes from a lucky family, and Kari, the avenger of Njal, is repeatedly said to be lucky.

Thus the foreshadowing elements in the sagas demonstrate that the situations in which a Nordic hero finds himself are largely beyond his control and that he must play the cards dealt to him by an essentially malevolent universe. The foreshadowing statements in the *Nibelungenlied,* however, are of a different type. Having in the first adventure described Kriemhild's dream of the falcon killed by two eagles (which is exceedingly like that of Thorstein in *Gunnlaugs saga*), the poet states that "the time came when she was wed to a very brave warrior, to that same falcon whom she had seen in the dream which her mother had interpreted for her. What terrible vengeance she took on her nearest kinsmen for slaying him in days to come! For his one life there died many a mother's child" (p. 19). Again in the third adventure the poet, speaking of Siegfried's desire to marry Kriemhild, states that from his bride "he was to receive much joy, yet also great distress" (p. 23). Nearly every adventure contains similar statements. However, these assertions of the disaster to come do not, like those in the sagas, attribute future catastrophes to fate but are instead presented as the natural results of the deliberate actions of the characters. Gunther wins Brunhild by guile, "though he had cause to rue it later" (p. 54); Siegfried is tormented by his passion for Kriemhild, "thanks to which, in days to come, the hero met a pitiful end" (p. 52); and "thanks to the wrangling of two women, countless warriors met their doom" (p. 118).

At only one point does fate enter the *Nibelungenlied*. Having been told by a mermaid that only the king's chaplain will return alive to Burgundy, Hagen tries to drown him in order to break the spell. The chaplain, however, escapes "by the hand of the Lord," and "this brought it home to Hagen that there would be no escaping the fate which the wild nixies had foretold" (p. 198). This incident, however, is unique in the poem and seems to have been included to intensify the portrait of Hagen's grim fortitude in the face of insurmountable odds rather than to convey the sense of cosmic doom which hangs over the Norse sagas. Hagen's fate and Kriemhild's and Gunther's are unavoidable, yes, but unavoidable because the characters have made them so, not because the Norns have preordained them.

The ultimate effect of destiny in the world of the Norse sagas is to endow the hero with a dignity and nobility which characters of the *Nibelungenlied*, even Rudiger, lack. For while Kriemhild and Hagen fight only each other, Gunnar in *Njals saga* and Kjartan in *Laxdœla saga* do not fight against men alone but also against their destinies, in fact against the common destiny of man. The Norse heroes, moreover, are sharply aware of their relation to fate and in this are perhaps superior even to Achilles, who defies fate by remaining at Troy yet seems hardly to recognize the consequences of his actions. And unlike Beowulf and Roland, these heroic Norsemen, at least the admirable ones, are also aware of the effects of their defiant heroism upon their families and comrades. They lack for the most part the *hubris* which so marks the individualistic heroes of other works of heroic literature.

A good deal of the nature of the Norse hero stems from the historical situation which produced the sagas. Iceland was settled mainly by independent Norwegian landholders who, rather than submit to the rule of the ambitious Harold Fairhair, who had set out to conquer the regional Norwegian kings and so bring all of Norway under his control, left Norway to make a new life on the recently discovered island. From 870 through 930 some fifty thousand settlers came to Iceland; by the end of the settlement period they had established the basic form of government which was to rule the island until the fall of the Commonwealth in 1264.

The form of self-rule created by the first settlers reveals clearly the character and temper of the Icelanders who are later to become the heroes of the sagas. The basic unit of local government was originally the *thing,* or assembly, a public meeting for debate and decision, attended at first by all the freemen of the area but largely controlled by those landholders whose possessions and influence made them the natural leaders of their districts. By 930 the *Althing,* or national assembly, had been formed to provide a common government and legal code for the entire island. The legislative power of the *Althing* rested in the hands of thirty-six (later forty-eight) *godar* (singular *godi*), who were the local leaders in charge of the pagan temples in their areas. These men in turn appointed thirty-six judges, who formed the judiciary. About 960, however, the court was divided into four Quarter Courts, each having jurisdiction over one-fourth of the island.

The individual *godi* was a person of considerable importance. He was both the temple-keeper, to whom taxes for the upkeep of the temple were paid, and the local secular authority. He was usually the chieftain of his district and was responsible for the protection of his *thingmen,* who were free to choose their *godi* and were obliged to support him in legislative and judicial quarrels and occasionally to accompany him to the *Althing.* The office of *godi* was hereditary but might be transferred, sold, or divided at the will of the *godi.*

The Icelanders thus created a form of government at once aristocratic and democratic, oligarchical and representative. It is the sort of system one would expect of a nation of free landowners who had chosen to move from their homeland rather than submit to the rule of an autocratic king. The chief feature of the Icelandic government, however, was that it provided only for the legislative and judicial functions: because of their zealous desire for personal liberty the Icelanders made no provision for an executive authority. The *Althing* might make laws and pass judgments, but it could not enforce them. Thus if a man were declared to be an outlaw by the *Althing* (a frequently imposed punishment), his sentence had to be imposed by the community at large. The *Althing* might well arbitrate a dispute and assess compensatory fines for killings, but it did not have the power to enforce its decrees, which all too often simply reflected the will of the strongest *godi* involved. Thus while this assembly form of government certainly left unhampered the personal freedom of its citizens, it could not adequately maintain law and order among a citizenry whose high regard for personal honor led naturally to deadly feuds among individuals and families.

In time, control of the *Althing* became a matter of bitter dispute among a few leading families. In the mid-twelfth century, only a half century before the time of the writing of the great family sagas, the balance of power among the *godar* was upset by the acquisition by several local chieftains of more than one *godord.* The greatest of these chieftains were the members of the Sturlung family, one of whom was the great Snorri Sturluson—not only a politician but also the age's most distinguished historian and poet, and perhaps its greatest saga writer—who was murdered by his own sons-in-law. The Sturlung Age was a time of confused loyalties and barbaric slaughter. Victory belonged to the strongest, but because of constantly shifting political alliances one family could win only temporary victories. Unchecked by central authorities, the carefully preserved individualism and integrity of the local chieftains led to anarchy in which treachery and murder replaced the heroic code of fair battle. In the end the king of Norway, after years of careful planning and intrigue, was able to gain control of all Iceland, and in 1264 the nation of independent farmers became tributary to the Norwegian throne.

The family sagas or Sagas of the Icelanders[4] with which this discussion is concerned were for the most part written during the thirteenth century, immediately following the Sturlung Age, but they deal with events of the so-called Saga Age, which extends from the end of the settlement period in 930 to about 1030, some thirty years after the Christianization of the island. The saga writers were thus looking back upon and writing about events some three hundred years before their own time, events which were grounded in history but which had become, again through the medium of oral transmission, at least partly legendary.

Students of the Icelandic sagas disagree about the degree to which these works reflect a continuing oral tradition, the advocates of the "free-prose" theory asserting that the stories were completely formed before they were set down in their present forms, the "book-prose" theorists that they were primarily the creations of individual authors. There are of course arguments to be advanced on both sides,[5] but because Icelandic history is relatively well documented for the period, a compromise position, that of the so-called Icelandic school, seems to be gaining influence steadily.

Avoiding the extremes of both free-prose and book-prose advocates, the members of the Icelandic school, principally Sigurd Nordal, Peter Hallberg, and G. Turville-Petre, maintain that the sagas are indeed the creations of individual writers but that these writers, far from creating their sagas *in vacuo,* in fact drew largely on oral tradition (particularly for customs and details of daily life), on written history and geography, and on skaldic verses. Most of the sagas can be shown to contain all three sources in various proportions. *Egils saga,* for example, records from oral tradition the resting place of Egil's remains; the ball game in which at the age of seven Egil kills an eleven-year-old child; and the astute psychological maneuvering by which Egil's daughter, Thorgerd, persuades the aged Egil to compose the *Sonatorrek,* a lament for his sons, and so postpone his suicide. From written history, though the exact sources are lost, the saga writer takes descriptions of Finnmark and the campaigns of Harold Fairhair and Hakon the Good. And *Egils saga* is filled with skaldic verses, principally those of Egil, too complex to have been preserved in oral tradition.

In short, we have in the composition of sagas a situation very like the one we have observed elsewhere: a poet looking back over several centuries combines legend and history, preserved largely in an oral tradition, to re-create for his own age the heroic tradition of his people. But because he himself is a product of his own age rather than the past, the poet interprets the past in terms of the present and so becomes not only a recorder of past times and values but their critic as well.

We will limit our discussion to three of the major sagas— *Egils saga, Njals saga,* and *Grettis saga*—not only because these three are the most famous and most accomplished works of their kind but also because they represent various stages in the development of the saga style and present, as does no single saga, a nearly complete range of saga situations and values. *Egils saga,* the earliest of the three, was probably composed in the period 1220–1225, perhaps by Snorri Sturluson himself,[6] and so is closest both to the historical tradition which it records and to the period of the great Icelandic historians such as Ari the Learned. *Njals saga,* written some fifty years later, shows a considerable movement away from the historical emphasis which *Egils saga* displays in its concentration on the lives of rulers and their intrigues and campaigns, toward a more literary form in which the conflicts and motives of the central characters become the main issues. In *Njals saga* a significant use is made of non-historical traditions, and the narrative style is much improved over that of the earlier saga. In *Grettis saga*, written early in the fourteenth century, one sees the conquest of folk tradition and literary values over the historical interests of the earlier saga writers.

By examining these three sagas in their proper chronological order, one can see, moreover, certain recurring themes and values which demonstrate, despite the changing style and emphasis, both the impact of the Saga Age upon that of the Sturlungs and the ways in which the old material was reshaped, with slightly varying emphases depending on the individual intentions of the three writers, into a commentary on the writer's age.

It is apparent that all three works reflect a firmly established code of heroic behavior based, as are all heroic codes, upon an exaggerated (at least to present-day readers) notion of the relative worth of personal honor and integrity, a concept closely related to the Icelander's fatalism. If a man cannot influence the events of his life, he can at least control his own reactions to those events; and from a heroic stand against outrageous fortune he can achieve a sense of personal integrity and a reputation which will be for both him and his progeny the only satisfaction he can gain from life. Thus honor, personal and family reputation, becomes the most valuable prize that the Icelandic hero can win for himself and the one gift he can pass on to his offspring.

This desire for honor, however, often results, as in the other heroic works, in a pride so fierce as to lead even the most levelheaded of men "beyond the bleak heroic necessity to excess—to chivalry."⁷ Thus the ordinarily sensible Gunnar in *Njals saga* chooses death at home rather than a dishonorable outlawry abroad and dies rather than force from the vindictive Hallgerd by an unseemly, demeaning act a few strands of hair with which to restring his bow. The sons of

Njal in the same poem accept death by burning rather than dishonorably ignore the obviously bad advice of their father. Flosi in *Njals saga,* although the fiery Hildigun has been unsuccessful in goading him, finally determines to burn Njal and his family alive when he fancies that Njal has impugned his virility and hence his honor. *Egils saga* deals with the efforts of three generations of the family of Kveldulf to take revenge, one of the requirements of the code of honor, against the Norwegian royal family for the slaying of Kveldulf's brother. Thorstein Dromund must travel to Constantinople to avenge his half-brother, and the struggle between Kari and Flosi resulting from the burning of Njal is not resolved until five years have passed, during which Kari pursues the burners to Orkney and Wales and finally makes a pilgrimage to Rome.

This tendency toward "chivalry" in even the most reasonable of the saga heroes becomes almost manic in the more hot-blooded characters, whose honor is likely to be offended by the most inconsequential actions. Because of a trivial argument over precedence in table seating, Hallgerd and Bergthora, Njal's wife, systematically have each other's servants killed until seven men lie dead; and Egil at one point gouges out an eye of a farmer whom he feels has not shown him sufficient hospitality. Grettir continually misuses his great strength and indeed kills a man (and, incidentally, his two brothers) who has offended him simply by throwing Grettir's coat into a bear's cave.

It is apparent, in fact, that there are in all the sagas, and especially in the three under discussion here, two attitudes toward the concept of honor: the justifiable pride which leads the hero to defy death to protect his family and the exaggerated sense of self-importance which causes him to bristle his crest at any slight, real or imagined, and without conscience to wreak havoc in his society in order to maintain his personal integrity.

The characters who reflect this opposition are usually presented, as in the Homeric epics, in close conjunction: Thorolf and Skallagrim, the younger Thorolf and Egil, Arinbjorn and

Gunnhild in *Egils saga;* Hoskuld and Skarp-Hedin, Njal and
Flosi in *Njals saga;* Atli and Grettir, Illugi and Grettir in
Grettis saga. Generally speaking, the first heroes in these
pairs are tactful, gracious men of whom society approves.
They have a fine sense of civic responsibility and so do everything in their power to avert the bloody feuds precipitated by
their headstrong companions. Thorolf through sheer ability
rises high in the service of Harold Fairhair, though in time he
becomes the victim of slander; the noble Arinbjorn is trusted
by King Eirik and is willing to oppose the fiery Queen Gunnhild to defend Egil. The saintly Hoskuld becomes a chieftain
and renounces the code which would require him to avenge his
father's death by killing Njal, who has adopted and befriended
him; Njal himself makes concession after concession to avoid
the violence and tragedy which he inwardly knows to be inevitable. Both Atli and Illugi in their tact and industry present
a strong contrast to Grettir, their quarrelsome, lazy brother.
Nor are these more civic-minded characters lacking in
heroism. Njal accepts his fate calmly and Hoskuld dies
blessing his murderers. Both Atli and Illugi, when pressed,
prove to be valiant fighters, and both die courageously and
defiantly.

Laudable as these men may be, however, they lack the
glamorous, though irresponsible, heroism of Egil, Skarp-Hedin,
and Grettir. And indeed the great scenes are those in which
the hero, like Achilles, goes "beyond the bleak heroic necessity
to excess"—Egil, the poet and pirate, drinking vast quantities
of beer and loutishly insulting the Norwegian rulers; Skarp-
Hedin skimming across the ice, axe in hand, at the battle of
Markar River, and at the burning hurling Thrain's jawtooth
into an enemy's eye; Grettir defying the burning eyes of
Glam's ghost. But as with Achilles, Beowulf, and Roland, the
necessary concomitant of this sort of heroism seems to be
social irresponsibility, a total disregard for the rights of others
and the welfare of the community. Thus Egil on his deathbed
contemplates throwing out his silver by the handful from the
Law Rock in hopes that the members of the *Althing* will
brawl over it; Skarp-Hedin's sardonic insults alienate the

chieftains whose support his family desperately needs; and Grettir's impetuosity, as well as his "ill-luck," results in his bringing tragedy to those who befriend him.

Thus again we find heroic and corporate values opposed, and again the writer's, in this case the writers', attitude toward them can be seen to be ambivalent. The more tactful, community-minded characters are certainly admirable; it is upon them that social stability depends, and they certainly cannot be said to be lacking in heroism. Yet they are to a degree compromisers: Thorolf supports the ambitious and jealous Harold, and Arinbjorn, the weak, hesitant Eirik; there can be no doubt that Kveldulf, Skallagrim, and Egil, despite their murderous ways, are justified in their resistance to the Norwegian tyrants. And Njal, despite his kindly efforts to avoid a tragic feud, is because of his reluctance to fight virtually powerless both against Mord and, ironically, against the impetuous members of his own family. Although the civic-minded chieftains have the highest ideals and motives, they are generally ineffective in preventing bloodshed and tragedy. Obversely, the great individualists, the Egils and Grettirs, are completely effective in accomplishing what they set out to do, but their actions result in pillage and destruction.

The style of the saga does not permit its author to obtrude upon the action, but there are indications that this opposition between heroic and corporate values is intentional and that it constitutes the poet's attitude toward his own time. The structure of the three sagas under discussion, and indeed of all the sagas, is strikingly similar. All of them begin one or more generations before the hero's time and, with the exception of *Egils saga*, extend well past his death. The opening sections of *Egils saga*, for example, establish in Thorolf and Skallagrim the opposition of values later to be developed in the younger Thorolf and Egil and trace the beginnings of the feud between the family of Kveldulf and the Norwegian royal house. The story of Gunnar, which dominates the first third of *Njals saga*, prefigures by the opposition of Mord and Gunnar the essential theme of the Njal story—the destruction of a man of good will by unscrupulous enemies. In the same way the opening chapters of *Grettis saga* trace in the family feuds, which result in the emigration of Grettir's forebears to Iceland, the background of violence against which Grettir's own story takes place. And the extended conclusions of both *Njals saga* and *Grettis saga* show plainly enough that the sins of the fathers are visited upon the sons; only after years have passed are the issues raised by the burning of Njal and the murder of Grettir settled.

Surely the purpose of this three-fold structure is not only to point out the deep roots and far-reaching effects of the struggle which occupies the main narrative but also to demonstrate its universality. All men, says the saga writer, are born into a world in which the most trivial accidents may grow into deadly feuds and even the noblest men may precipitate bloody quarrels—a world dominated by a malevolent fate against which no man, no matter what his course of action, can prevail and from which he can gain no victory save in a final heroic defiance.

The sagas, then, present two possible ways of life in such a world: that of the chieftain who works, sometimes at the expense of his own honor, for the stability of society and that of the individualistic hero whose sole motive is to preserve his integrity, even at the expense of the corporate good. The first is all too often destroyed by the violence he attempts to curb; the second too often becomes an outlaw, forced by his violent nature to live apart from the community. In the end, however, both are destroyed by the fate that controls all men, and the struggle in which they take part continues unabated after their deaths.

It is not surprising that such a conflict of values should be the chief theme of the sagas. By the early thirteenth century, Iceland was already in its death throes; the Sturlung Age had demonstrated the failure of both the *Althing* and the heroic code of the past to keep order. Barbaric cruelty, broken pledges, arson, murder, and the most hideous excesses of savagery had replaced the honorable, though stern, code of the settlement period. "Time after time there are reports of forged letters sent out to entice one's enemy to destruction. The breaking of promises is common. There are instances of chieftains who have the men of their adversaries maimed; a hand or foot is cut off, or they are castrated. The practice of having concubines was widespread, even among the clergy, and evoked bitter complaints from the church leadership about immoral ways of life."[8]

The saga writers in examining the legends and bits of written history that preserved the traditions of the Settlement Age must have been struck by the contrast of this earlier period with their own corrupt time. Granted that the sagas were written primarily for the entertainment of the original settlers' descendants, who still lived in considerable isolation on their scattered farms and looked to these long tales simply for diversion during the long winters, the writers nevertheless demonstrate a serious awareness of the contrast between past and present values and of the failure of the heroic code to provide a way of life in their own time. It is this failure which is defined by the two opposing groups of characters. The older values, the ideals to which the Icelandic Commonwealth was dedicated, are presented in the Njals, the Thorolfs, and the Arinbjorns—those figures whose heroic efforts are devoted to the welfare of the community. The extreme egocentric heroism of the Sturlung Age can be seen, on the other hand, in the Skallagrims, the Skarp-Hedins, and the Grettirs—those men who have allowed their concept of personal honor to blind them to the devastating effects of their actions upon the community in which they live.

Both sets of figures, of course, represent idealizations; we are here dealing with archetypes, and even those saga heroes who have historic counterparts have been shaped at least to some degree by tradition and their authors into representative types. Yet the saga writer is careful to avoid character, and hence value, distinctions so sharp as to force either himself or his reader to make a choice: Njal, for all his wisdom and consideration, is ineffective in stemming the tide of violence which eventually overwhelms his family; and Skarp-Hedin, despite his willful irresponsibility, dies with his father rather than offend him. Like the other heroic writers we have examined, the saga writer is not didactic, and if he sees the desire for personal power and glory as a great danger in his own society, he, like his ancestors, also sees that man can reach fulfillment only in terms of individual heroism.

The thirteenth-century saga writer counterbalances the two great threats to his own society—the unchecked individualism of the Sturlung Age and the movement toward an expedient union with Norway. Like Homer, he sees the strengths and weaknesses of both positions, and like Homer, he cannot choose absolutely between them. That choice, for Scandinavia as for Greece, was a matter for history to determine: in swearing their allegiance to the Norwegian throne in 1264, the Icelandic farmers forsook the principle of independence which had brought them to Iceland over three hundred years before and which had determined the shape of their heroic literature.

CHAPTER SEVEN

The Arthur Legend

It is a pity that there exists no single literary document from the Arthurian tradition to match the other works we have examined. For while we have a plenitude of chronicles and romances dealing with the great British hero and his court, there is no one poem or history, with the possible exception of the *Historia Regum Britanniae* of Geoffrey of Monmouth, which stands at the end of the oral and the beginning of the written tradition and which brings together, as does the *Iliad*, all the themes and motifs of the oral tradition to balance and judge them in the context of a new age. Yet it is worthwhile to examine the Arthurian materials, and particularly Sir Thomas Malory's *Morte Darthur*, as a kind of summary and conclusion since they demonstrate, when taken as a whole, many of the principles inherent in all heroic literature.

One major factor which must be considered in dealing with the development of the Arthur story is that upon emerging from the oral tradition it takes the form of two sharply distinguishable literary forms. Our information concerning the historicity of Arthur and the origins of the tales concerning him comes basically from two types of sources: the works of chroniclers, whom we would call historians, and the body of Celtic folklore that has come down to us. The first evidences are thus both historical and mythological; they become the springs from which flow two streams of Arthurian tradition, the chronicle and the romance.[1]

Most modern students agree that there was indeed a historical Arthur, though there was never a King Arthur of the type celebrated in the later legends. The Arthur from which the legend grew was almost certainly a military leader of the Britons in their wars against Saxon invaders during the fifth century. Strangely enough, the most contemporaneous account of the period, the *De Excidio et Conquestu Britanniae* written by the monk Gildas about 540, does not mention Arthur by name, though it does describe the battle of Badon Hill, later to be associated with Arthur. The name *Arthur* first appears in a Welsh poem, *Gododdin*, written presumably by the poet Aneirin in the early seventh century. In this elegy for the British who fell in the northern battles against the Angles, it is said of one hero that he "glutted black ravens on the rampart of the fort, though he was not Arthur," that is, that he provided the ravens with dead bodies, though not to the extent that Arthur had. The importance of this single allusion is its demonstration that in not much more than a hundred years after Mount Badon, the name of Arthur had spread to the north of England and was already a name to conjure by.

The first account of Arthur by a historian, however, is given in the *Historia Britonum*, written about 800 by the Welsh priest Nennius. Nennius relates fully the coming of the Saxons and the first years of Saxon victories; eventually he describes how one Arthur, who fought "along with the kings of the Britons, but was himself a leader of the wars" (*cum regibus Brittonum, sed ipse erat dux bellorum*), fought twelve victorious battles, apparently throughout England, against Octa, the son of Hengist, culminating in the victory at Mount Badon, where Arthur alone slew 960 of the enemy.

The term *dux bellorum* has created considerable dissent among historians. It may indicate simply that Arthur was commander in chief of the combined British forces or, as R. G. Collingwood has maintained,[2] that he was a member of a Roman family, elected to be *dux bellorum*, who successfully organized and maintained a kind of mobile cavalry troop which could effectively combat the Saxon infantry. Whatever his rank, however—and whatever it is, it is not that of king— his importance as the savior of the Celtic defenders is clear.

Something of the aura of legend that had come to surround the native hero in the three-hundred-odd years since the battle of Mount Badon can be seen in Nennius's accounts of the number of Saxons he killed and of two miracles concerning him. These two miracles, set down in a section of Nennius's work called *De Mirabilibus Britanniae*, recount how a heap of stones in south Wales is topped by a stone bearing the footprint of Arthur's dog, Cabal, which though moved always returns to its place, and how the grave of Arthur's son Anir varies in length each time it is measured.

The *Annales Cambriae*, or *Annals of Wales*, which were probably compiled in the early ninth century, contain two interesting allusions to Arthur. The first, dating the battle of Mount Badon at 516, asserts that at that battle Arthur bore the "cross of our Lord Jesus Christ on his shoulders three days and three nights"; this reference thus establishes his Christianity.

The second of the two statements in the *Annales Cambriae* is of great importance to the legend. In 537, we are told, occurred the "battle of Camlann, in which Arthur and Medraut fell." There can be little doubt that Medraut is the Mordred of later legend, that the story as we know it is already beginning to take shape, and that it was from the beginning given a tragic ending. Certainly the circumstances of the battle of Camlan, whatever they were, must have been as familiar to the author's contemporaries as those of Mount Badon.

These early records demonstrate beyond doubt that the legend of Arthur, whether or not he ever existed in fact, continued to grow in the years following the Saxon wars. It is possible, moreover, to see even in the passing remarks of these chronicles something of the shape of the later legend. If we accept, at least for the moment, the theory of R. G. Collingwood as being substantially correct, we can reconstruct a historical situation which in many ways parallels the legendary account of Arthur's career.

After its first successful thrusts the Saxon advance was halted in south Britain by an elected professional soldier-leader named Arthur who had realized the military advantages of cavalry against unmounted troops and had organized a mobile mounted force, the effectiveness of which he had demonstrated in battles throughout England. Then in one furious charge at Mount Badon this Arthur broke the back of the Saxon forces and established a peace which lasted for some thirty years. However, internal disputes, presumably stemming from a struggle for power, broke out among the Britons; these disputes culminated in the battle of Camlan between Arthur and his rival Medraut in which both were killed. The Saxon attacks were renewed, and the leaderless British gradually retreated into the peripheries of the island, into Cornwall and Wales, and across the Irish Sea, consoled only by the memories of their past greatness and of the leader who had for a time turned back the advancing hordes of Saxons.

Although other early chroniclers furnish us with bits and pieces of the growing tradition of Arthur's greatness, it is with Geoffrey of Monmouth that we have the real beginning of Arthurian literature. In fact, "no work of imagination," writes E. K. Chambers, "save the *Aeneid,* has done more to shape the legend of a people than the *Historia Regum Britanniae,*"[3] for in that work is found for the first time the skeleton of the whole legend of Arthur to which previous chroniclers had only alluded. We have the familiar story of Arthur's birth—how Uther fell in love with Igerna, wife of the Duke of Cornwall, and how through a substitution instituted by Merlin, Uther was accepted by Igerna as her husband and bore Arthur. On coming to the throne at age fifteen Arthur conquers not only the Saxons but the neighboring kings as well and, after a period of peace, most of Europe. He marries Guinevere and establishes a great medieval court. Then, challenged by the authority of Rome, the great king embarks upon a second European expedition, leaving his kingdom under the regency of his queen and his nephew, Mordred. Word comes to him en route that his regents have betrayed him, and he turns back to England. There he defeats Mordred in a series of battles during the last of which he himself is apparently mortally wounded but is carried to the Isle of Avalon to be healed.

However, Geoffrey's contribution to the Arthurian tradition lies in more than his setting down for the first time a coherent account of the mass of legend which presumably had been accumulating for six hundred years, ever since the battle of Camlan. Geoffrey also places the legend in the setting it is to assume from his time onward. Arthur is no mere elected cavalry leader but a great king presiding over a chivalric court so magnificent that all the courts of Europe copy its manners and dress. His enemies are no longer bands of Germanic invaders but the kings of Europe and even the Emperor of Rome himself. Arthur's knights are products of the new chivalry whose deeds on the battlefield and in tournaments and whose behavior at court are inspired and refined by the hope of finding favor in their ladies' eyes.

One of the first and most influential works based on Geoffrey's *Historia* was the *Roman de Brut,* or *Story of Brutus,* the mythical founder of England, by the Norman poet Wace, a work which is in the main a French verse paraphrase of Geoffrey's Latin prose. Written in 1155, Wace's *Brut* was apparently composed for Eleanor of Aquitaine, whose husband, Henry II of England, had assumed the throne the year before, to supply that noble lady with some knowledge of the nation over which she was to rule. Although it follows Geoffrey closely, Wace's lively poem omits some details— particularly Merlin's prophecies—and adds some new material. He emphasizes, as would be expected of a court poet, the courtly elements of the tale, especially the chivalric figure of Gawain; accounts for the creation of the Round Table, at which all might sit equally; discusses the habits of the *conteurs,* or storytellers; and enlarges greatly on Geoffrey's descriptions of banquets and festival occasions.

Though he is writing in the chronicle tradition, Wace casts the legend in what is to become perhaps its most fitting and most habitual form, the vernacular metrical romance. Geoffrey's rather pedestrian Latin is, despite its subject matter, rather heavy going, but Wace's short verses are sprightly: he is fond of exclamations and rhetorical questions and in a number of scenes substitutes direct for indirect discourse. Through Wace's poem the Arthur story became the source of many later romances.

The Arthurian chronicle tradition did not, however, end with Wace, for Wace's *Brut* in turn became the source of the first English metrical chronicle, Layamon's *Brut*. Just as Wace's *Brut* reflected the chivalric courtly tradition, so Layamon's poem is close in spirit and method to the Anglo-Saxon heroic tradition. Layamon's chief expansions of his source are found in his descriptions of battles, just as those of Wace appear in his descriptions of life at court. Layamon is, wherever possible, dramatic and graphic, particularly in the use of direct discourse and figurative speech. Arthur himself is seen as a rough warlord, not a courtly gentleman. Layamon's additions are also important to the development of the legend. Fairies are present at Arthur's birth to bestow gifts on him; the Round Table is founded not, as in Wace, simply as a means of bestowing equality of station on Arthur's knights but because a brawl makes necessary such a device. Arthur dreams before his return to England of the doom that lies before him, and at the end he announces to Constantine, his successor, that he will indeed return to help the English.

With Layamon the early chronicle tradition of Arthur comes to an end. Traced from its spare and illusive beginnings, it manifests a consistent pattern of development in which the major concern is historical. The chroniclers are writing what is to them the history of England, a history made up of all sorts of what seem to us to be extraneous elements, but always aimed at presenting the Arthur story within the context of the growth of the English nation. Thus Geoffrey, Wace, and Layamon present the whole story of Arthur from his birth through his tragic defeat and miraculous departure to Avalon. They are not concerned with particular episodes of the legend for their own sakes nor with the adventures, however marvelous, of individual knights. For this kind of story we must turn to the tradition of Arthurian romance.

The Arthurian tradition in romance, properly speaking, begins with Chrétien de Troyes, the first writer of romances. Its roots, however, lie so deeply embedded in Celtic folktales, both oral and written, that some knowledge of these early tales is necessary to an understanding of the tradition in which Chrétien is working.

It seems certain, first of all, that the romance tradition does not evolve from that of the chronicles but that both go back to a common body of Arthurian legends which grew slowly among the Welsh during the centuries following their expulsion from England by the Saxon invaders. This body of legends is composed of at least two elements, a fact which accounts for our being able to distinguish between a chronicle strain and a romance strain in the development of the Arthur story.

There was, as one would expect, a glorification of the deeds of the historical warrior, a magnification of the *dux bellorum* of Mount Badon into a great king whose conquests encompassed nearly all of Europe and who numbered among his followers the greatest knights the world has ever seen. But, as we have noted, in this process of development from history into heroic literature, another element, mythology, often influences and in fact becomes so entangled with the facts of history that myth and history are well-nigh inseparable. It is not surprising, therefore, that the Arthur story came to incorporate many of the incidents and characters of older Celtic myth and legend. For example, both the names and attributes of Sir Gawain and Sir Lancelot can be traced to Celtic sun gods, and the bridge from which Gawain falls in Chrétien's *The Knight of the Cart* is descended from numerous references in Celtic mythology to crossings into the otherworld.

In the development of the Arthur legend exactly the same division of scholarly opinion exists that we have noted in dealing with the sources of other heroic works. A group of Arthurian scholars usually called Celticists claim Celtic folklore to be the mainspring of virtually all the elements of later Arthurian stories, wherever and whenever they appear, having been transported from Wales to France and thence throughout Europe by Breton *conteurs*.[4]

Such a theory, of course, leaves little room for originality to those writers of the later Arthurian tradition, and it is exactly on this issue that the so-called Inventionists take their stand. Despite the argument of the Celticists that any approach to the Arthur story which is not purely historical is based only on "subjective reactions," the Inventionists maintain that the critic has a right to go beyond the confining limits of source study, especially since in so many instances the derivations put forward by the Celticists are extremely tenuous. J. D. Bruce, for instance, says bluntly that he is convinced that the debt of the romancers to Celtic sources has been "greatly exaggerated and that personal invention was the most important factor in the creation of these romances. . . . The authors of these romances were primarily poets, not transcribers of folktales, and it seems strange that scholars should so often have imputed to them the strictest accuracy in following imaginary folktale sources."[5]

As we have said before, sanity lies somewhere between the two extremes. It is certain that a great many, perhaps the majority, of the elements of plot, character, and theme that grace the later Arthurian romances derive from Celtic oral tradition. However, the ultimate sources of these materials are at best so conjectural and the lines of transmission at once so vague and so tangled that one must admit the possibility of original additions at a hundred junctures.

But whatever the sources of Chrétien de Troyes may have been, it is with his romances that the Arthurian romance tradition properly begins. Although a number of Chrétien's poems and translations have been lost, five, possibly six, have come down to us: *Erec and Enide; Cligés; Lancelot; Yvain*, or *The Knight of the Lion; Perceval*, or *The Story of the Grail;* and perhaps *William of England*. The first five are parts of the so-called Matter of Britain, that subject division of the medieval romance which contains the Arthur stories; they deal with the adventures of individual Round Table knights. *Erec and Enide*, for example, tells of the courtship, marriage, and marital trouble of one Erec, son of Lac. The romance begins "in spring, at Easter" at the court of King Arthur in Cardigan. Erec, having undertaken the quest of the White Hart—a typical beginning to such a story—fights a joust on behalf of Enide, the daughter of a poor vavasour, and brings her to Arthur's court to be his bride. However, once married, he neglects to keep up his reputation in arms and upon discovering from Enide that he is generally thought to be uxorious sets out on a series of adventures to regain his reputation. These adventures comprise the greater part of *Erec and Enide,* and though they appear at first sight to be rambling and digressive, they actually form a pattern in which Erec can be seen to regain, step by step, his self-confidence and reputation. Following his trials he returns briefly to Arthur's court before going on to claim his own throne upon the death of his father.

It will be seen that in *Erec and Enide,* Chretien is not in the least interested, as were the chroniclers, in presenting a history of the rise and fall of Arthur's kingdom. His major purpose is to present a series of adventures, very loosely bound together, involving a particular hero of Arthur's court. The court itself is simply a point of departure from which the knight sets forth, and its main function seems to be to set the scene of the story in Logres, Arthurland, and to assure us of the hero's worth by assigning him a place at the Round Table.

Chrétien is interested in more than the adventures of his heroes and heroines, however. His emphasis, as a matter of fact, is on their psychology—on the motivations of their actions and particularly on their reactions toward falling in love. Indeed it can be said that his greatest contribution to the Arthurian tradition is his treatment of the romantic affairs of the knights of the Round Table, an aspect of the legend which the chroniclers with their emphasis on the whole history of the court failed to consider. *Erec and Enide* and *Yvain* deal with the marital state of the knight—the first with Erec's uxoriousness, the second with Yvain's neglect of his role as husband and as protector of his estate. *Cligés,* which is at least partly indebted to the Tristan legend, concerns the dilemma in which Fenice finds herself when she is married by force to a man she does not love.

Lancelot, however, deals with what is generally called courtly love and introduces into the Arthurian legend the adulterous union of Lancelot and Guinevere. Courtly love was brought into the south of Europe in the eleventh century in the form of Arabian lyrics which extolled a relation between the sexes totally alien to the traditional notions of sexual behavior in western culture. This new religion of love, for indeed it did become in time a kind of religion, elevated "the lady" to a pinnacle of adoration and abased her knightly suitor to the position of a servant. No longer was a woman to be regarded, as she was in the classical and early medieval periods, as simply a childbearing, homekeeping drudge but instead as the delicate, refined, charming, and infinitely desirable heroine of later romantic fiction. Her suitor, having succumbed at first sight to her charms, immediately experienced all the ills of unrewarded passion—sleeplessness, lack of appetite, apathy, disinterest in everyday affairs, and, worst of all, despair in the face of his unworthiness even to approach this new-found goddess. Yet in time he might well accomplish his suit; and since the lady was already married, probably to a man she did not love, the almost inevitable result of the courtly love affair was adultery.

The practice of courtly love thus resulted in a paradox of values. The young knight, once relieved of his initial "malady of love," practiced every kind of virtue to "stonden in his lady grace." Brave, devout, generous, polite, accomplished in all the arts of courtly conduct, he was transformed by love from callow youth into chivalric manhood. Yet, human nature being what it was and is, the platonic relationship of lady-master and knight-servant could not endure, and the two found themselves involved in an intimacy totally opposed to accepted mores of Christian society. Thus courtly love, despite its civilizing effects upon the rough world of the medieval court, was condemned by the Church both because it usually culminated in an adulterous union and because it involved a reversal of the roles of the sexes which the Church advocated in Christian marriage. Though there is much in *Lancelot* to suggest that Chrétien himself did not approve of courtly love, it is the first of the romances to deal with the phenomenon, and its influence was such that it largely set the subject matter and the style for following generations of romancers.

In time the Arthurian romance spread well beyond France. There are extant romances dealing with Arthur's heroes in Spain, Portugal, Italy, Germany, Holland, the Scandinavian countries and, of course, England. Like Chrétien, later romancers made little or no attempt to view their material from any sort of historical perspective, to see the rise, flowering, and downfall of a civilization. To tell an entertaining story was their principal aim. Later writers, as we shall see, were to incorporate the romance material into the framework of the chronicle story; but before we can properly deal with them, we must examine one group of Arthurian romances which because of its independent origin and development must be set off from the general stream of the romance—that dealing with the adventures of the knights of the Holy Grail.

The origins of the Holy Grail legend are very difficult to ascertain, and indeed Arthurian specialists differ more widely here than on any other matter. The Grail first appears in the last of the romances of Chrétien, *Perceval,* or the *Conte del Graal,* in which, as in *Lancelot,* Chrétien professes simply to be rewriting a book given to him by a patron, Philip of Flanders. The *Conte del Graal* deals for the most part with the adventures of the youthful Perceval, who leaves his widowed mother to enter training at Arthur's court. In the course of an early adventure Perceval encounters two men fishing, one of whom directs him to a nearby castle for shelter. There he finds an old man lying on a couch and surrounded by four hundred retainers. A strange procession enters carrying a bleeding lance, a ten-branched candlestick, a *graal* (a large dish), and a silver carving plate. This same procession accompanies each course of the meal that follows.

Perceval, remembering the advice of a tutor, refrains from inquiring about what he sees, sleeps, and awakes to find the castle deserted. Later he learns that had he asked the meaning of what he saw, the maimed Fisher King, who had directed him to the castle, would have been healed.

From this strange and illusory tale stems the Grail branch of Arthurian romance. One of the first "continuators" of Chrétien, Robert de Boron, provides us with the mythological antecedents of the *graal* which occupies such an important place in Chrétien's *Conte del Graal*. This vessel, says Robert, is none other than the Holy Grail itself, the vessel which was first used by Christ at the Last Supper and later to catch the blood flowing from his wounds. After the crucifixion the Grail was given by Pilate to Joseph of Arimathea, who was instructed by Christ in a vision to form a companionship to guard the holy chalice. After a series of great trials Bron, Joseph's brother-in-law, called the Rich Fisher, carried the Grail westward, presumably to Glastonbury in England, leaving Joseph to die in his own land.

It is not certain, of course, that Robert's *Joseph d'Arimathie* derives directly from Chrétien's *Conte del Graal;* both writers may be working independently from lost sources. Yet certain correspondences suggest that both poems indeed concern the same subject; and Robert, writing perhaps ten years after Chrétien, clearly identifies Chrétien's *graal* with the most sacred of all Christian relics.

The casual reader may therefore be surprised to learn that heated controversy has raged over the source and origin of the vessel. The main reasons for the argument are that Chrétien's narrative is unfinished and that its *graal* references are vague and mysterious, perhaps deliberately so. Three principal theories of origin, as well as a number of lesser conjectures, have arisen concerning the source of the Grail legend.

There are, as one would expect, a number of scholars, particularly J. D. Bruce, who maintain that the Grail was *ab origine* a part of the Christian legend which Chrétien inherited and to which he added "the character of the Grail knight and the conception of the quest."[6] According to this theory, the procession at the mysterious castle is a Eucharistic procession, much like that used in Byzantine ceremonies, and the lance is that with which the centurion Longinus pierced the side of our Lord. Jessie Weston, on the other hand, has suggested that the Grail and the lance were sexual symbols which were originally part of the initiation rites of a mystery religion, part Christian, part pagan.[7] The Celticists, as one would guess, see in the Grail vestiges of Celtic myth; R. S. Loomis, for example, observes a number of parallels between Bran, the Fisher King, and King Bron of Welsh legend and traces the various articles of the Grail procession to Celtic prototypes.[8]

Whatever its origins, however, the Grail enters the mainstream of Arthurian literature as a Christian symbol, and from Chrétien onward the quest of the Holy Grail rapidly develops into a distinct branch of Arthurian tradition. We shall see how later writers amalgamated the quest into the history of Arthur's court, but some hints of its later role can be discerned even this early in the tradition. Certainly the high holiness of the Grail presents a startling contrast to the cult of courtly love which dominates most of the romances. Both are religious, both entail a kind of mystic vision, both make great demands upon their devotees; yet they are directed toward entirely different aims—the one toward a spiritual union with God, the other toward an all too physical union with the beloved. It was inevitable that the Arthur story, indeed chivalry itself, should come to contain both Grail and courtly love; it was also inevitable that these elements should conflict and thus contribute to the downfall of the high civilization of the Round Table.

Three streams, then, fed the great river of the fully developed story of the rise and fall of Arthurian chivalry: the early histories of the chroniclers, the chivalric romances of the Matter of Britain, and the legend of the Holy Grail. For hundreds of years each ran its own way, concerned only with its own themes and devices and touching the others only in occasional references to Arthur's court, the traditional starting point of chivalric adventures.[9]

I have dwelt upon the early development of the Arthur story at length in order to make a single point: while the Arthurian tradition does not boast a single great heroic work which summarizes and interprets all the themes of a lost oral tradition, its earliest written forms nevertheless exhibit the same elements—history, legend, and myth—we have noted elsewhere in heroic literature. Furthermore, we can assume that these elements, which were diffused in the chronicle, courtly, and religious traditions, all originated in a single oral tradition. These conflicting elements seem to me to find their resolution in Sir Thomas Malory's *Morte Darthur,* a work which, although removed by centuries from the oral tradition, pulls together the scattered threads of meaning inherent in the early works and weaves the story's definitive garment.

It may be argued that Malory, like Homer, was conscious of both the traditions and their conflicts since the *Morte Darthur* everywhere demonstrates his care in removing the contradictions and inconsistencies which he found in his sources. He carefully reconstructs the entire chronology of the story in thematic rather than strictly chronological order, eliminating long sections which are irrelevant to his narrative and thematic structure and making additions where he needs them. He makes consistent the actions of characters such as Gawain and Morgan le Fay whose conduct in his sources is at times incomprehensible. And the very fact that he manages to create order and unity out of the chaos of the tradition seems to demonstrate that from the outset he envisioned his task as that of a unifier rather than a simple redactor or translator.

Nor is there much doubt that Malory wrote for the age in which he lived.[10] That he apparently spent a good deal of his adult life in prison for such crimes as attempted murder, rape, extortion, theft, and cattle rustling has been over-emphasized. As C. S. Lewis says, we have only the legal charges laid against him, not his defense, and the terms of these charges may not have meant in the fifteenth century what they mean today.[11] We must recognize also that Malory was a conservative country aristocrat, almost certainly autocratic in temperament and probably crusty as well, rather like Squire Western in *Tom Jones*. His misdemeanors may thus very well have stemmed from a somewhat exaggerated sense of the importance of his position and rank and would not have been regarded by himself or by his class as at all "criminal."

Seen from this point of view, the *Morte Darthur* is the very sort of book such a man might write, for superficially it is a justification of the conservative and aristocratic way of life, a lament for the passing of the old ways. Certainly its first editor, William Caxton, sensed this quality in the book when he wrote that it was printed so that "noble men may see and lerne the noble actes of chyvalrye, the jentyl and vertuous deeds that somme knyghtes used in tho dayes."[12] And indeed Malory had good reason to proclaim in his own time the chivalric code of the past which he still espoused, even though he may not have lived up to it, for chivalry in the mid-fifteenth century had lost its operative value as a military and political standard. To be sure, the early Tudor monarchs sponsored revivals of the rituals of chivalry, its jousts and tourneys and feasts, but in this "Indian summer of English chivalry"[13] the ideals and practices of knighthood had very little effect upon the conduct of the politically sophisticated new English aristocracy.

It is not surprising, then, that a Tory military agrarian such as Malory should set out certainly not to revive but at least to reassert in the midst of change the ethical code of chivalric behavior which had produced in former years a Black Prince and a Henry V. One can in fact see much of this intent in the *Morte Darthur*. A famous passage in which Arthur lays down at the very formation of his kingdom the principles which are to govern the new chivalry is of Malory's own composition and indeed sets the stage for much of the action to follow. The knights are enjoined

> never to do outerage nothir morthir, and allwayes to fle treson, and to gyff mercy unto hym that asketh mercy, upon payne of forfiture [of their] worship and lordship of kynge Arthure for evirmore; and allwayes to do ladyes, damesels and jantilwomen and wydowes [socour:]

162

strengthe hem in hir ryghtes, and never to enforce them upon payne of dethe. Also that no man take no batayles in a wrongefull quarell for no love ne for no worldis goodis.[14]

Throughout the book, as C. S. Lewis says, is "an enforced reverence not only for courage (that of course) but for mercy, humility, graciousness, and good faith."[15] In fact, when one examines the first four long sections of the *Morte Darthur*—those dealing respectively with the formation and unification of Arthurian Britain, Arthur's war with the Roman Emperor Lucius, the early exploits of Sir Lancelot, and the coming to court of Sir Gareth—one sees at every hand Malory's emphasis on the evolution of the ethical code outlined in Arthur's charge. Whereas the older, pre-Arthurian knights of the first tale are crude, warlike bullies, much given to rape and senseless murder, the representatives of the new chivalry are unfailingly kind, courteous, and fairminded and so represent the code introduced by Arthur. Whereas early in the book Gawain kills a damsel simply by "myssefortune" and Pellinore rapes Torre's wife, Lancelot later refrains from punishing Phelot's wife even though she has aided her husband in attempting to kill him, and he scrupulously denies any unlawful alliance with the queen.

In short, throughout his book Malory seems to be defining the same dichotomy of values we have seen elsewhere in heroic literature, though, as would be expected, with an emphasis peculiar to his own time and situation. The pre–Round Table knights, the early Gawain, for example, represent the old, individualistic, chivalric values, those of Achilles or Roland or the Arthur of Geoffrey and Layamon and of the fourteenth-century alliterative *Morte Arthure*. They act by no standards other than those demanded by their sense of honor. The Round Table civilization created by Arthur and best exemplified by Lancelot is an attempt to create a new kind of chivalry only hinted at in the sources, a chivalry based on corporate values, in which the virtues of the romance tradition—the sense of honor and the integrity, courage, and prowess—would remain but would be diverted into socially useful standards "through which the confusing instincts of nascent chivalry [might] be focused and preserved."[16]

Yet the theory that Malory wrote the *Morte Darthur* simply to revive a waning chivalry or even simply to contrast pre- and post-Arthurian chivalry will not explain the whole book, no matter how well it may clarify its first half. For the Arthurian story as Malory received it is a record not of the success of chivalry in creating a workable standard of ethical behavior but of its failure to do so. However morally right the faithful Lancelot may appear, his liaison with Guinevere is later to destroy the court. However noble Arthur's charge to the youthful knights may be, their later feuds and acts of disloyalty split the kingdom. However high-minded the first enthusiasm for the Grail quest appears, its pursuit is to destroy many of the finest knights. For all its glorious beginnings, the *Morte Darthur*, like the chronicles, ends in dissolution and failure, unredeemed by even the merest hint of hope for the future.

Thus while Malory does emphasize the practical, ethical code of chivalric life and so deemphasizes to a degree certain elements of medieval courtliness of which he probably disapproved—the rituals of courtly love and the Cistercian mysticism of the Vulgate *Grail*, for example—he does not change, as indeed he could not have changed, the tragic nature of the story. Nor does he, even though he may have wished to do so, transform the legend into an ethical panacea for his own time.

It therefore seems to me that while the *Morte Darthur* does indeed rehearse the way of life "in tho dayes," it does not in the least attempt to glorify it. And this aspect of the work Caxton also sensed, for he warns the reader that it records both the deeds "by whyche they [Arthur's knights] came to honour, and how they that were vycious were punysshed and ofte put to shame and rebuke"; and he enjoins the reader to "doo after the good and leve the evyl."[17] The whole *Morte Darthur* thus rests upon a paradox of which its writer was most surely conscious and which his own changes do much to heighten. On the one hand, the chivalric life is seen by

Malory, as by the writers of romances, to encompass the highest ideals of conduct that man can envision. By the practice of "courage . . . , mercy, humility, graciousness, and good faith" man can raise himself from barbarism and create a society based on justice and virtue. Yet man is in the end only man; the old primitive standards and values continually reassert themselves, and even the most nobly conceived society cannot survive the failings of human nature. Despite Arthur's efforts, Gawain will be Gawain, and even the noble Lancelot is trapped by a confusion of values inherent in the chivalric code. Thus chivalry, even at its best, is doomed *ab origine* to failure; and the Round Table, shot through with immorality and civic strife, must in the end crumble.

There is no need to rehearse at length either the intricate plot of the *Morte Darthur* or the many specific changes Malory makes in adapting his immediate sources. The point is that by careful revision he develops the seeds of tragedy which had lain dormant in the legend in the chronicles' bitter recitals of the last days, in the debilitating effects of courtly intrigue described in the romances, and in the endless, frustrated wanderings of the Grail knights. His chief means of defining the difference between the selfish, individualistic values of the older chivalry and the corporate values of the new, and at the same time indicating the failure of both to create a permanent society, is a systematic alteration of his sources to bring to the forefront the feud between the houses of King Lot and King Pellinore and the adulterous love affair of Lancelot and Guinevere. Both of these themes had certainly existed in his immediate sources but had been buried beneath innumerable accounts of quests and tourneys. I have described elsewhere in some detail how Malory winnowed out these themes to give form and unity to his book,[18] but since they are obviously used also to emphasize the dichotomy of values which eventually splits the court, some further discussion is justified here.

King Lot of Orkney, one of the recalcitrant kings of Britain whom the newly crowned Arthur must subdue in order to maintain his throne, is married to Arthur's half-sister, Morgause. Not realizing her identity, Arthur takes her to bed and so begets Mordred, whose treachery is eventually to destroy the kingdom. During these early wars King Lot is killed in battle by King Pellinore, and Lot's fiery sons, particularly Gawain, Gaheris, and Agravaine, swear vengeance against the house of Pellinore, "for he slewe oure fadir kynge Lott" (p. 102). A series of killings follows: Pellinore is "shamefully slayne by the hondys of sir Gawayne and hys brothir, sir Gaherys" (p. 810); Morgause is killed by Gaheris after she becomes the mistress of Lamorak, Pellinore's son; Lamorak is ambushed and murdered "felounsly" by "Gawayne and his bretherne" (p. 688); Patryse is poisoned by Pynel "bycause of hys kynnesman sir Lamorakes dethe" (p. 1049). Finally, after Lancelot accidentally kills Gareth, the youngest of the Orkneys, Gawain's demand for vengeance forces Arthur to exile Lancelot and brings on the civil war which eventually destroys the court. Thus, although Gawain and his brothers yearly pledge fealty to the Round Table and to the whole society of which they are a part, they continue to maintain the older code of individual and family honor and in so doing split the court and destroy it.

Likewise Lancelot, though he is the exemplar of Arthur's new corporate chivalry, contributes to the downfall of the court by failing, despite his best efforts, to renounce another set of values inherited from the past, those of courtly love. Here again in choosing, often against his better judgment, to remain the obedient lover-servant of the queen, as the code of courtly love demanded, Lancelot is pledged to an individualistic set of values which cannot help conflicting with the communal values of the court. He must rescue Guinevere, whose adultery is a proven fact, from execution even though he surely knows that this action will help destroy the civilization which he has sworn to help maintain. By consistently emphasizing the role of the Lancelot-Guinevere affair in the destruction of the Round Table, Malory brings to the fore, as in his handling of the Lot-Pellinore feud, the fundamental division of individual and corporate values inherent, though unexploited, in his sources.

Significantly, the roots of this conflict between individual and corporate values may well lie in the fact that as in the other works we have examined, the figure of the king is descended from history while those of the knights are derived from myth. Again, there is little doubt that the Arthur of the chronicles, whatever his later glories, was in fact a professional Celtic cavalry leader who fought against the Saxon invaders in the early sixth century and that in the romances the principal actors—the Lancelots, Gawains, Morgans, Merlins—and a great number of incidents—including the Grail quest, the abduction of Guinevere, and the courtship of Gareth—are descended from Celtic myth.[19]

Here again the pattern repeats itself. As the story develops, we move from history to legend to legend-fortified-by-myth to epic, and in the process the focus shifts from legend to myth and hence from king to hero. As the legend, and with it the sense of national importance, grows, as the court, whether *comites* or Round Table, is established, the figure of the king takes on a greater shape but a lesser function. Arthur can no longer ride out like Lancelot or Gawain; he must preside over his court. Hygelac cannot leave Geatland to pay his obligations to Hrothgar; Beowulf must go. Charlemagne weeps that Roland must command the rearguard, yet he knows his own place is with the main force. The king must support the image of the nation, exemplifying the character of the whole: in becoming an archetype he becomes the center from which all action originates, though he himself may not take part in that action; in creating and representing the glory of an ideal he loses much of his own glory and in time even ceases actively to defend the ideal. At the outset of the Grail quest, in which, significantly, the knights choose to pursue their individual destinies rather than to uphold the common tasks of the court, Arthur laments the passing of the civilization he has framed and over whose dissolution he must preside:

> "Now," seyde the kynge, "I am sure at this quest of the Sankgreall shall all ye of the Rownde Table departe, and nevyr shall I se you agayne hole togydirs, therefore ones

shall I se you togydir in the medow, all hole togydirs!
Therefore I wol se you all hole togydir in the medow of
Camelot, to juste and to turney, that aftir youre dethe men
may speke of hit that such good knyghtes were there, such
a day, hole togydirs." (p. 24)

Thus the king—Agamemnon, Charlemagne, Arthur—
first in creating his nation and later in exemplifying its
image, must leave its active defense to lesser, or at any rate
to less idealized, figures, to Achilles or Roland or Gawain, the
figures of myth. It is clear, moreover, that these are indeed
less idealized men; though they are heroes, they are essentially subjects rather than kings and as such bear the
faults of general humanity, particularly an overweening
pride, a kind of *hubris,* in their own ability. They are essentially egotistical; their own reputation, their own honor is
to them of supreme importance. Unlike the kings, they never
place national safety or national honor above their own safety
and honor. Hence they sacrifice nation to self and bring down
upon *comites* and Round Table the tragic results of their pride.
Lancelot, according to Arthur, ever trusted too much in his
arms, and Gawain's personal vendetta against Lancelot helps
split the Round Table; despite Oliver's counsel, Roland refuses until it is too late to blow the horn to summon Charlemagne and assure a French victory; Beowulf, having refused
the Geatish throne at a time when he could have saved the
nation, pridefully attempts in his old age a task beyond him,
and when he dies, he leaves the Geats unprotected against
the Swedes.

The king in heroic literature presides over a crumbling, or
at least a crisis-stricken, nation and becomes therefore a
figure of tragedy. His virtues, which are also the values of
the nation he represents, are thus apparent in times of national calamity and defeat. This is, of course, partly a matter
of literary emphasis; tragic kings are a better subject for
literature than are universally successful ones: we and
Homer are more touched by the fall of Priam than by the
victories of Agamemnon, and the death of Hygelac is the
thematic center of *Beowulf,* the one event which shapes the

whole poem. Even Charlemagne at the end is observed as brooding and painfully unwilling to continue his campaign against the heathens.

In short, the king, who begins as the idealization of a legend, in the end comes to represent the values of his nation in defeat; and the hero, who begins as the humanization of a myth, in the end represents only himself, as his glory is overcome by his self-destructive pride. Paradoxically, the mythical hero destroys the legendary king.

But legends endure as myths do not, and the corporate values of kingship eventually replace the individual virtues of the hero. Thus, although Arthur is a shadowy, inactive figure, his image remains to the Englishman a symbol of his own best self—an idealist, a man of vision, a creator of stable and beneficent government; in times of adversity stalwart, patient, and enduring; a man created by destiny to rule, yet doomed to destruction by the passions of those who do not share his vision or understand the nature of his creation.

I had best comment on the nature of the universe as reflected in Malory's book lest by omission I seem to qualify my former statement that heroic values of the type we have been discussing cannot be reflected in a work underlain by Christian precepts. Certainly no one would dispute the presence of Christianity in the *Morte Darthur*. The sense of sin weighs heavily upon Lancelot, as upon all the Grail knights; as I have said elsewhere, one of the three great causes of the downfall of the court is its failure to assimilate into its concept of chivalry the standards of religious life necessary to the creation on earth of the *Civitas Dei*.[20] Indeed Charles Williams, the most genuinely creative of those modern writers who have reworked the Arthur story as vehicles for twentieth-century ideas, sees the Grail quest as central to the whole story and its failure to unite chivalric civilization and Christianity as its major theme.

Even so, it is clear that Malory makes considerable changes in the religious content of his sources and that in his hands the failure in religion becomes only one, and probably the least important, cause of the downfall of the Round Table civilization. For example, the immediate source for his Book 6, *The Tale of the Sankgreall,* is the thirteenth-century *La Queste del Saint Graal,* a part of the Old French Vulgate Cycle. This long, heavily theological work, written probably by a Cistercian monk, undergoes severe modification; although Malory is careful to preserve its essentially religious nature, he greatly alters its mystical and homiletic tone by deleting most of its long theological sections, largely the commentaries of hermits, in an effort to fit the Grail quest more closely into the whole history of the court. The source for his first book is the *Suite du Merlin,* a part of the post-Vulgate cycle; it too is heavily Grail-oriented, and here again one may observe his careful shifting away from the emphasis on the "foreshadowings of the Grail."[21] He thus consistently reduces both the amount and the kind of Christian material that he inherited.

It is possible, moreover, that in so altering his sources, Malory used the religious materials not only to frame one of the causes of the downfall of the Round Table but also as a means of reinforcing the division of values that underlies the Lot-Pellinore feud and the adultery of Lancelot and Guinevere. The chivalric oath quoted above, one of Malory's great contributions to the Arthur story, is in general terms a statement of Christian principles. Certainly the Christian ideas of forgiveness and charity as well as "mercy, humility, graciousness, and good faith" are inherent in the oath and thus form the basis of Arthur's new chivalry. But, as we have said, this is a peculiarly Arthurian ideal of conduct, readily accepted by the newer knights, especially Lancelot who, even so, fails to live up to it, but flagrantly violated by Gawain and his brothers who, unmoved by its spirit, relentlessly pursue the older chivalric values.

My point is that Malory's knights, though not his king, are in the last analysis motivated by chivalric and individualistic rather than by Christian and corporate values and that the *Morte Darthur* is essentially concerned with the failure of

Christian chivalry rather than that of Christianity itself. True, Lancelot's adultery and Gawain's pursuit of revenge are from the Christian point of view sinful, but Malory approaches them primarily as flaws in the chivalric system and not as offenses against religion. The *Morte Darthur* is thus not a "Christian epic" in the sense that *The Faerie Queene* and *Paradise Lost,* in which the poet judges every action solely by Christian standards, are; Malory's book is able to concentrate, as do the superficially Christian *Song of Roland* and *Nibelungenlied,* upon the failure of heroic values in a context of a chivalric society in which the Christian doctrines of forgiveness and charity are shown to be essentially inoperative as ethical standards.

The *Morte Darthur,* then, despite the fact that it draws upon written rather than oral sources, provides our final demonstration of the idea that at the heart of much heroic literature lies a distinction—sometimes clear-cut, at other times complicated by the particular intentions of the author or the demands of the times—between the historical king, the representative of a new corporate scheme of national values, and his mythical captain, the staunch defender of the old heroic values of personal integrity and honor. Save in the *Odyssey,* where a single hero exemplifies both attitudes in the course of his career, this dichotomy of values ends, or as in the *Iliad* almost ends, in the tragic destruction of either hero or state or, more frequently, of both.

I have said before that heroic literature is essentially realistic even though it deals with the materials of fantasy. For at its best, say in the *Iliad,* the epic deals reflectively and objectively with one of the great temptations of the Western mind, the desire to find in the past a golden age when issues were more clear-cut and conduct more heroic, when society was simpler and more stable, when the gods did indeed walk the earth. In viewing that golden age, heightened and glorified by legend and myth passed through an oral tradition, the heroic writer is able to see in it its best and most enduring values, but he is also able to observe it against the background of history and of his own age and so is able to judge it. Hence the heroic work involves an equilibrium, a perilous balance between the old and the new, the heroic and the commonplace, the individual and the state. In such poetry resides an enduring record of man's best efforts to understand the paradoxical nature of the world in which he lives.

$\mathcal{N}otes$

Chapter One: THE ILIAD

[1] Cf. C. M. Bowra, *Tradition and Design in the Iliad* (Oxford: Clarendon Press, 1930). I am deeply indebted throughout this chapter to Bowra's masterful discussion.

[2] W. F. Thrall and Addison Hibbard, *A Handbook to Literature*, rev. C. Hugh Holman (New York: Odyssey Press, 1960), p. 175.

[3] It has been suggested that the poem as we have it was composed by a group of fifth-century rhapsodes, the so-called Sons of Homer.

[4] Bowra, *Tradition and Design*, pp. 15–17.

[5] Erich Bethe, quoted by Susanne Langer, *Philosophy in a New Key* (Cambridge, Mass.: Harvard University Press, 1942), p. 177 n.

[6] The best and most up-to-date summary of the historical background is probably that of Denys Page, *History and the Homeric Iliad* (Berkeley: University of California Press, 1966).

[7] Like all questions of early Greek chronology, the date of the fall of Troy is much disputed. The best account of the problems concerning the period for the general reader is probably Joseph Alsop's *From the Silent Earth* (New York: Harper and Row, 1962), a gifted amateur's synthesis of the technical arguments of the specialists.

[8] G. S. Kirk, *The Songs of Homer* (Cambridge: Cambridge University Press, 1962), p. 14.

[9] These are the famous Linear B tablets first translated in the early 1950s by Michael Ventris. An account of this exciting discovery is given in Alsop, *From the Silent Earth*, pp. 30–37.

[10] Kirk, *The Songs of Homer*, pp. 152–53.

[11] Rhys Carpenter, *Folk Tale, Fiction, and Saga in the Homeric Epics* (Berkeley: University of California Press, 1962), pp. 75–77.

[12] Robert Graves, *The White Goddess* (New York: Vintage Books, 1960), passim, and *The Greek Myths*, 2 vols. (Harmondsworth, Middlesex: Penguin Books, 1955), 2:288.

[13] T. L. Webster, *From Mycenae to Homer* (London: Methuen, 1958), pp. 69–71, 79–82.

[14] See Richard M. Dorson, "The Eclipse of Solar Mythology," *Journal of American Folklore* 68 (1955): 393–416.

[15] R. S. Loomis, *Celtic Myth and Arthurian Romance* (New York: Columbia University Press, 1927), p. 47.

[16] Graves, *The White Goddess*, p. 420.

[17] Loomis, *Celtic Myth*, p. 40.

[18] Cf. Joseph Campbell, *The Hero with a Thousand Faces* (New York: Pantheon Books, 1949).

[19] Bowra, *Tradition and Design*, p. 204.

[20] E. V. Rieu, trans., *The Iliad* (Harmondsworth, Middlesex: Penguin Books, 1950), p. 400.

[21] There is of course a good deal of dissension as to whether Homer could actually have written the poem, that is, composed it in writing rather than totally in his head. It seems to me that although Homer's style is based almost entirely on the oral formulas, genealogies, and other devices of orally composed poetry (as they quite naturally would be, given his training), the balanced structure and unity of the whole poem, in short the internal evidence, points to the kind of composition possible only with a written, and hence manageable, text. The fact that Webster (*From Mycenae to Homer*, p. 272) and Bowra (*Homer and his Forerunners* [Edinburgh: Nelson, 1955], pp. 10–14) believe that the poem was composed in writing while Denys Page calls such an opinion "impossible" (*History and the Homeric Iliad*, p. 158) demonstrates the controversial nature of the external evidence.

[22] It would seem that this incident, in which Menelaus and Paris fight a duel for Helen, would fall most naturally in the first days of the war.

[23] Graves's eccentric theory is set forth in his introduction to his translation of the *Iliad*, *The Anger of Achilles* (New York: Doubleday, 1959).

[24] Both Bowra (*Tradition and Design*, pp. 234–50) and H. M. Chadwick (*The Growth of Literature*, 3 vols. [Cambridge: Cambridge University Press, 1932–1940], 1:74) agree on these qualities as distinguishing the heroic temperament.

[25] Bowra, *Tradition and Design*, p. 244.

[26] Ibid., pp. 215–17.

[27] Except perhaps for the vestigial totemism of "ox-eyed Here" and "bright- [hence owl-] eyed Athene." Cf. ibid., pp. 219–21.

[28] Ibid., p. 217.

[29] Graves, *The Greek Myths*, 1:48.

[30] Ibid., p. 27.

[31] Graves, *The White Goddess*, p. 416.

[32] Graves, *The Greek Myths*, 2:269.

[33] Graves, *The White Goddess*, p. 540.

[34] *Iliad*, p. 458.

Chapter Two: THE ODYSSEY

[1] E. V. Rieu, trans., *The Odyssey* (Harmondsworth, Middlesex: Penguin Books, 1946), p. 25. Subsequent quotations from the *Odyssey* are from this translation.

[2] Howard W. Clarke, *The Art of the Odyssey* (Englewood Cliffs, N.J.: Prentice-Hall, 1967), p. 6.

[3] Ibid.

[4] There is no way, of course, to prove that Homer did indeed "invent" the device of beginning a story *in medias res*. However, since, as I believe, he was able to compose the *Odyssey* in writing (see chap. 1, note 21) he would have been able, as previous writers working strictly within an oral tradition presumably would not have been, to have invented such a complex form of narrative construction. It is certainly noteworthy in this connection that the flashback technique is never used in purely oral tales.

[5] Clarke, *The Art of the Odyssey*, p. 6.

[6] Alfred Lord Tennyson, "Ulysses," in *The Poetic and Dramatic Works of Alfred Lord Tennyson*, Cambridge ed. (New York: Houghton Mifflin, 1898), p. 88.

[7] *Iliad*, p. 365.

[8] W. B. Stanford, *The Ulysses Theme* (Oxford: Basil Blackwell, 1954), p. 93.

[9] Clarke, *The Art of the Odyssey*, p. 64.

[10] Ibid., p. 51.

[11] Ibid., p. 54.

[12] Ibid., p. 48.

[13] Stanford, *The Ulysses Theme*, p. 8.

[14] Graves, *The Greek Myths*, 2:366.

[15] Stanford, *The Ulysses Theme*, p. 9.

[16] Graves, *The Greek Myths*, 2:366.

[17] Carpenter, *Folk Tale, Fiction, and Saga in the Homeric Epics*, p. 156.

[18] Stanford, *The Ulysses Theme*, p. 10.

[19] Graves, *The Greek Myths*, 2:366.

[20] Stanford, *The Ulysses Theme*, p. 74.

[21] Clarke presents a detailed account of Telemachus's transformation in *The Art of the Odyssey*, pp. 30–44.

Chapter Three: BEOWULF

[1] Jan de Vries, *Heroic Song and Heroic Legend* (London: Oxford University Press, 1963), p. 10.

[2] Ibid., p. 20.

[3] Peter Hunter Blair, *Roman Britain and Early England* (New York: W. W. Norton, 1963), p. 247.

[4] Our chief authority for the history of Northumbria during the period of the Anglo-Saxon invasions is the Venerable Bede, a man, to quote the period's leading modern historian, "of alert and curious mind, in a position to be acquainted with those who knew the facts" (F. M. Stenton, *Anglo-Saxon England* [Oxford: Clarendon Press, 1947], p. 5). It is clear from Bede's account that although the Saxon menace did not become serious in northern England until the second half of the sixth century, there did develop at the very end of that century two strong Anglian kingdoms in Northumbria—Deira to the south and Bernicia to the north— and that these two kingdoms had by that time absorbed the "considerable number of small, independent kingdoms ruled by British dynasties" (Peter Hunter Blair, *An Introduction to Anglo-Saxon England* [Cambridge: Cambridge University Press, 1956], p. 39), as well as a number of smaller Anglo-Saxon units. During the reign of the warlike Æthelfrith (ca. 593–616) Bernicia was able to "win control over Deira and so to create the kingdom of Northumbria" (Blair, *Introduction*, p. 45). Under Æthelfrith the English were able also to conquer a portion of the Scottish lowlands and to defeat the Britons at Chester, thus extending their control to the shores of the Irish Sea. Æthelfrith's personal triumphs, however, were short-lived, for in 616 he was defeated in battle by Edwin, the Deiran heir, who not only became king of a unified Northumbria but, as successor to Rædwald, the Anglian king, also became "overlord of all the English peoples south of the Humber" (Stenton, *Anglo-Saxon England*, p. 79).

Edwin's short rule (616–632) is important here because in his conduct of office we can clearly observe, perhaps for the last time in Northumbria, the personal, as distinct from national or tribal, allegiance which Tacitus insisted was the "dominant characteristic of early Anglo-Saxon society" (Blair, *Roman Britain*, p. 247). As Sir Frank Stenton says, Edwin's confederation was "of a barbarian type"; "its basis was the mere allegiance of individuals"; and "in character and environment [Edwin] belonged to the world depicted in Old English heroic poetry." "Like other heroes, he had travelled far as an exile, and had known his life to depend on the conflict between honour and interest in the mind of a protector. He secured his father's kingdom through the help of a stronger king, and made himself in time the lord of other kings. He moved over the country surrounded by retainers ready to give their lives for him" (Stenton, *Anglo-Saxon England*, p. 79).

Edwin thus "stands in history as a great king of the age of

national migrations rather than as the predecessor of Offa or Alfred" (Stenton, *Anglo-Saxon England*, p. 80). Despite its extent, his kingdom was destroyed in 632 by a coalition of Cadwallon, the British king of Gwygnedd in Wales, and Penda, later to become king of Mercia. After a brief series of sharp internecine struggles, Æthelfrith's son, the saintly Oswald, defeated Cadwallon and became king of a reunited Northumbria.

There followed another brief period of Northumbrian expansion in which Oswald was able to strengthen his position in the South through marriage and also to conquer the British stronghold of Edinburgh. Oswald's career and the political supremacy of Northumbria, however, came to a sudden end with his defeat by the heathen King Penda of Mercia in 641. Penda, unlike Oswald, apparently had little or no feeling for national unity or consolidation but instead obviously valued personal renown, and Northumbria again fell into its two historic sectional divisions. Within a few years, however, Oswiu of Bernicia defeated the invading Penda in a last stand somewhere near modern Leeds and for a time became overlord of Mercia and the southern kingdoms which had never acknowledged Penda. But soon Wulfhere, Penda's son, was able to wrench from Oswiu his southern holdings, and after six years of struggle by their successors, the Northumbrians gave up any further attempts to annex territories south of the Humber, concentrating instead upon their Pictish enemies to the north until their defeat at Nechtanesmere in 685 ended northward expansion.

With the ascension of Aldfrith in 685 Northumbria entered a period of considerable stability. A learned man as well as a talented soldier, Aldfrith encouraged learning among the clergy and at the same time "re-established his ruined kingdom nobly, though within boundaries narrower than before" (Stenton, *Anglo-Saxon England*, p. 88). When he died in 704, the succession to the Northumbrian throne became so confused that during the eighth century, "out of 15 Northumbrian kings, five were dethroned, five murdered; two abdicated, and only three held the crown to their deaths" (R. W. Chambers, *Beowulf: An Introduction*, 3d ed. [Cambridge: Cambridge University Press, 1963], p. 324). Despite this turmoil, the reign of Aldfrith had been so effective that the first third of the eighth century, the time of the *Beowulf*-poet as well as of Bede, was the golden age of Northumbria, notable for its art, architecture, and scholarship.

During the same period Mercia was also enjoying a period of political consolidation under Æthelbald and Offa, who successively ruled that country for eighty years and under whom the southern kingdoms were either annexed to Mercia or "came under strong Mercian influence" (Blair, *Introduction*, p. 53).

[5] C. L. Wrenn, ed., *Beowulf with the Finnsburg Fragment* (Boston: D. C. Heath, 1953), p. 37.

[6] Blair, *Roman Britain*, p. 43.

[7] Ibid., p. 239.

[8] Ibid., p. 242.

[9] J. R. R. Tolkien, *Beowulf: The Monsters and the Critics* (London: Oxford University Press, 1958), p. 29.

[10] A. G. Brodeur, *The Art of Beowulf* (Berkeley: University of California Press, 1959), p. 234.

[11] R. K. Gordon, trans., *Beowulf*, in *Anglo-Saxon Poetry*, Everyman's Library (London: J. M. Dent and Sons, 1926), p. 52.

[12] Friedrich Klaeber, *Beowulf and the Fight at Finnsburg*, 3d ed. (Boston: D. C. Heath, 1950), p. 211.

[13] Gordon, *Beowulf*, p. 53.

[14] Ibid.

[15] Adrien Bonjour, *The Digressions in Beowulf* (Oxford: Basil Blackwell, 1950), p. 31.

[16] John Leyerle, "Beowulf the Hero and King," *Medium Aevum* 34 (1965): 89.

[17] Gordon, *Beowulf*, p. 50.

[18] Ibid., p. 61.

[19] Margaret Murray, *The God of the Witches* (Garden City, N.Y.: Doubleday, 1960), pp. 165–66.

[20] E. K. Chambers, *The Mediaeval Stage*, 3 vols. (London: Oxford University Press, 1903), 1:95.

[21] M. B. McNamee, "*Beowulf*—An Allegory of Salvation?" *Journal of English and Germanic Philology* 59 (1960): 190–207.

[22] Marie Hamilton, "The Religious Principle in *Beowulf*," *PMLA* 61 (1946): 309–30.

[23] See especially D. W. Robertson, "The Doctrine of Charity in Mediaeval Literary Gardens," *Speculum* 26 (1951): 24–49; R. E. Kaske, "*Sapientia et Fortitudo* as the Controlling Theme of *Beowulf*," *Studies in Philology* 55 (1958): 423–57; and Morton W. Bloomfield, "Patristics and Old English Literature: Notes on Some Poems," *Comparative Literature* 14 (1962): 36–43.

[24] Brodeur, *The Art of Beowulf*; Dorothy Whitelock, *The Audience of Beowulf* (Oxford: Clarendon Press, 1951).

[25] Klaeber, *Beowulf and the Fight at Finnsburg*, p. xlix.

[26] H. M. Chadwick, "Early National Poetry," in *The Cambridge History of English Literature*, vol. 1 (Cambridge: Cambridge University Press, 1940), pp. 30–34; H. M. Chadwick, *The Heroic Age* (Cambridge: Cambridge University Press, 1912), pp. 49–53; F. A. Blackburn, "The Christian Coloring in *Beowulf*," *PMLA* 12 (1897): 205–25.

[27] Blackburn, "Christian Coloring," p. 225.

[28] R. K. Gordon, trans., *Judith*, in *Anglo-Saxon Poetry*, Everyman's Library (London: J. M. Dent and Sons, 1926), p. 358.

[29] R. K. Gordon, trans., *Andreas*, in *Anglo-Saxon Poetry*, Everyman's Library (London: J. M. Dent and Sons, 1926), p. 233.

[30] Gordon, *Beowulf*, p. 69.

[31] Whitelock, *The Audience of Beowulf*, p. 98.

[32] Charles Kennedy, *The Earliest English Poetry* (London: Oxford University Press, 1943), p. 88.

[33] Brodeur, *The Art of Beowulf*, p. 204.

[34] Klaeber, *Beowulf and the Fight at Finnsburg*, p. li.

[35] Gordon, *Beowulf*, p. 54.

[36] Tolkien, *Beowulf: The Monsters and the Critics*, p. 285.

[37] Klaeber, *Beowulf and the Fight at Finnsburg*, p. xlix.

[38] R. H. Hodgkin, *History of the Anglo-Saxons*, 3d ed., 2 vols. (London: Oxford University Press, 1952), 1:232.

[39] See E. R. Dodds, *The Greeks and the Irrational* (Berkeley: University of California Press, 1951), pp. 1–27.

[40] Klaeber, *Beowulf and the Fight at Finnsburg*, p. xxx.

[41] Wrenn, *Beowulf with the Finnsburg Fragment*, p. 41.

Chapter Four: THE SONG OF ROLAND

[1] For recent summaries of the development of the two schools of criticism see Charles A. Knudson and Jean Misrahi, "French Medieval Literature," in *The Medieval Literature of Western Europe*, ed. John H. Fisher (New York: New York University Press, 1966), pp. 125–90; and Urban T. Holmes, Jr., "The post-Bédier Theories of the Origins of the *Chansons de Geste*," *Speculum* 52 (1955): 72–81.

[2] Jan de Vries, *Heroic Song and Heroic Legend* (London: Oxford University Press, 1963), p. 26.

[3] Ibid., p. 36.

[4] Urban Holmes, *A History of Old French Literature* (New York: F. S. Crofts, 1948), p. 103.

[5] Ibid., p. 71.

[6] *Song of Roland*, ll. 199–200. The translations in the text are mine.

[7] Bowra, *Tradition and Design*, p. 2.

[8] See Jean Rychner, *La Chanson de Geste* (Geneva: E. Droz, 1955).

[9] Joseph Bédier, quoted by George Fenwick Jones in *The Ethos of the Song of Roland* (Baltimore, Md.: Johns Hopkins Press, 1963), pp. 2–3.

[10] De Vries, *Heroic Song and Heroic Legend*, p. 29.

[11] Jones, *The Ethos of the Song of Roland*, p. 181.

[12] Dorothy L. Sayers, trans., *The Song of Roland* (Harmondsworth, Middlesex: Penguin Books, 1957), p. 19.

[13] Jones, *The Ethos of the Song of Roland,* p. 101.

[14] Ibid., p. 102.

[15] Ibid., p. 38.

Chapter Five: THE NIBELUNGENLIED

[1] It will be noted that in this brief résumé I am using the name forms of the *Nibelungenlied.* While differences in the name forms of the various early versions of the tale are important in tracing its development, they can be confusing to the nonspecialist; since they are of no real importance to my argument here, I have avoided them.

[2] Lord Raglan, *The Hero* (New York: Vintage Books, 1956), pp. 182–83.

[3] A. T. Hatto, trans., *The Nibelungenlied* (Harmondsworth, Middlesex: Penguin Books, 1965), p. 24. Subsequent quotations from the *Nibelungenlied* are from this translation.

[4] Daniel Bussier Shumway, trans., *The Nibelungenlied* (Boston: Houghton Mifflin, 1909), pp. xxvii, xxviii.

[5] As with the *Song of Roland,* critical opinion is divided. One school of thought is dominated by the genealogical approach of Andreas Heusler's *Nibelungensaga und Nibelungenlied,* which attempts to trace the poem's development through a maze of sources, extant and hypothetical. The other school, represented by Friedrich Panzer's *Das Nibelungenlied,* rejects the genealogical approach and assigns a high degree of originality to the poet, who, according to Panzer, made use of a number of motifs readily available in the literature of the period.

[6] Presumably the popular legend that Attila met his death at the hands of a captured German girl led to his identification as the husband of Kriemhild. Full assimilation of the Siegfried myth and the historical fall of the Burgundians did not, and indeed could not, come until the role of Kriemhild had been changed from her brothers' protector to their enemy.

[7] It is possible to argue either that Gunther does not actually compel Siegfried to swear that Gunther was "the first to enjoy [Brunhild's] lovely person" or that the terms of the oath are so stated by Gunther that Siegfried, who did not actually "enjoy her lovely person," may comfortably take the oath. In either case Gunther is carefully avoiding the fact that Siegfried did actually subdue Brunhild and took from her the girdle and the ring.

[8] Hatto, commentary in *The Nibelungenlied,* p. 314.

[9] This last action demands some further explanation. The

older legends state that Kriemhild instructed Ortlieb to strike Hagen, thus causing Hagen to kill the child and so strike the first blow in her battle with him. But Bloedelin's slaughter of the Burgundian squires, itself an act of horror, apparently made the sacrifice of Ortlieb unnecessary, and critics have thus wondered why the poet chose to include what appears to be a garbled version of the original action. The answer seems to me to lie not in the principle, too often cited in such cases, that the poet had to include in one form or another every single element of the traditional story but in the way he did in fact use such materials. Here, having bribed and cajoled Bloedelin into attacking the squires, Kriemhild deliberately has Ortlieb brought to Etzel's table, knowing that Hagen will upon hearing the news of Bloedelin's attack instinctively turn on Ortlieb and kill the boy in front of his father. Thus she insures Etzel's active support in her vendetta: her sacrifice of her son seems to be deliberately calculated to win over Etzel and is typical of her cold-blooded campaign of revenge.

[10] See, for example, Hatto, commentary in *The Nibelungenlied,* p. 334.

Chapter Six: *THE ICELANDIC SAGAS*

[1] John Keats to George and Thomas Keats, 21 December 1817, in M. B. Forman, ed., *The Letters of John Keats* (London: Oxford University Press, 1947), p. 72.

[2] The nature and extent of the effect of the conversion upon Icelandic thought and literature are hotly debated by the specialists, and the reader is directed to G. Turville-Petre, *Origins of Icelandic Literature* (Oxford: Clarendon Press, 1953) and Stefan Einarsson, *A History of Icelandic Literature* (Baltimore, Md.: Johns Hopkins Press, 1957) for general discussions. My own statement, it should be understood, is a purely literary opinion. For example, in the famous 132d chapter of *Njals saga,* the burners, having expressed their amazement at the preservation of the bodies of Njal and Bergthora, the radiance of Njal's countenance in death, and the crosses branded upon Skarp-Hedin's body, carry the bodies to church in proper Christian fashion. However, upon hearing the news of his foster father's death, Thorhall immediately swears vengeance upon the burners. As Einarsson says, "Even in Christian times fate did not relax her grip" (p. 132), and though the sagas may at times reflect Christian sentiments, they are essentially "the memories of a great heroic heathen society and reflect its spirit" (p. 131).

[3] Jean I. Young, ed., *The Prose Edda of Snorri Sturluson* (Berkeley: University of California Press, 1964), p. 44.

[4] The sagas are often conveniently divided into those of ancient, more recent, and contemporary times. The family sagas belong to the second of these groups.

[5] For a summary of these arguments and a bibliography see Paul Schach, "Old Norse Literature," in *The Medieval Literature of Western Europe* (New York: New York University Press, 1966), pp. 270–71.

[6] For a discussion of the date and authorship of the poem see the translation by Gwyn Jones, *Egils Saga* (Syracuse, N.Y.: Syracuse University Press, 1960), pp. 16–23.

[7] J. R. R. Tolkien, "Ofermod," in *The Tolkien Reader* (New York: Ballantine Books, 1966), p. 20.

[8] Peter Hallberg, *The Icelandic Sagas*, trans. Paul Schach (Lincoln: University of Nebraska Press, 1962), p. 31.

Chapter Seven: THE ARTHUR LEGEND

[1] For a comprehensive, up-to-date treatment of the development of the Arthur story the reader is directed to R. S. Loomis, ed., *Arthurian Literature in the Middle Ages* (Oxford: Clarendon Press, 1959).

[2] R. G. Collingwood, *Roman Britain and Its English Settlements* (Oxford: Clarendon Press, 1937), pp. 321–24.

[3] E. K. Chambers, *Arthur of Britain* (London: Sedgwick and Jackson, 1927), p. 20.

[4] Thus in *Arthurian Tradition and Chrétien de Troyes*, R. S. Loomis sets out to demonstrate that every character, every incident in Chrétien's romances can eventually be traced to a Celtic source, generally a mythological one. For example, after stating with commendable restraint that "a very considerable portion" of four of the romances of Chrétien is "of Celtic origin" (*Arthurian Tradition and Chrétien de Troyes* [New York: Columbia University Press, 1949], p. 467), Loomis goes on to identify the chief elements of the French poems, their characters, narrative patterns, and incidents, as being drawn from Celtic folklore, thus leaving Chrétien only a few proverbs, names, and rhetorical passages. The chief difficulty of these scholars in irrefutably maintaining their position lies, as one would expect, in the lack of written Welsh sources. They are thus driven to written Irish materials, where all too often the parallels are not exact enough to be totally convincing.

[5] J. D. Bruce, *The Evolution of Arthurian Romance*, 2 vols. (Baltimore, Md.: Johns Hopkins Press, 1923), 1:iv–v.

[6] Ibid., 1:251.

[7] Jessie Weston, *From Ritual to Romance* (New York: Doubleday, 1957), pp. 65–80.

[8] Loomis, *Celtic Myth and Arthurian Romance*, pp. 144–50.

[9] The first attempt at unification, however incomplete and faltering, comes with a collection of early thirteenth-century prose romances called the Old French Prose Vulgate Cycle or, usually, simply the Vulgate Cycle. Of enormous length, this group of romances is almost certainly of multiple authorship, having been composed by a number of French monks sometime between 1210 and 1230. The cycle proper consists of five romances, generally called "branches." The three original branches are the *Lancelot*, the *Queste del Saint Graal*, and the *Mort Artu*, which derive essentially from the romance, the Grail, and the chronicle traditions respectively. The other two branches are generally agreed upon to be later additions to the work—the *Estoire del Saint Graal*, which tells the early history of the Grail and which the author claims to be a copy of a book given to him by Christ Himself in a vision; and the *Estoire du Merlin*, which consists of a prose version of Robert de Boron's *Merlin* plus a "historical" sequel by an anonymous author and a preliminary to the *Mort Artu* recounting the early history of the court. Another and more faithful prose redaction of Robert's poem, however, exists in the Huth manuscript, where it is followed by a "romantic" continuation generally called the *Suite du Merlin*, which is probably part of a Grail-oriented, post-Vulgate cycle sometimes called the *Roman du Graal*.

These six works, the five branches of the Vulgate Cycle and the *Suite du Merlin*, taken together form the first partially unified Arthurian saga incorporating in its various parts the narrative framework of the chronicles, the adventurous tales of the romancers, and the religious mysticism of the Grail writers. Though composed by diverse hands, the Vulgate Cycle exhibits considerable unity; we cannot doubt that the composer of the *Lancelot* deliberately prefigured in his works events which were to take place in the works of his followers: the coming of Galahad in the *Queste* is predicted in the *Lancelot*, for example, as are the final wars between Arthur and Lancelot and between Arthur and Mordred. And despite noticeable differences in tone and manner among the three original branches, the characterization remains relatively stable throughout the long work. Lancelot, for example, is here raised to the place of primacy among the Round Table knights.

[10] Despite the work of William Matthews, which substitutes a Thomas Malory of Yorkshire for the Thomas Malory of Newbold Revel, I am assuming here the traditional identification to be the correct one.

[11] C. S. Lewis, "The English Prose Morte," in *Essays on Malory* (Oxford: Clarendon Press, 1963), p. 10.

[12] William Caxton, "Preface" to the *Morte Darthur*, in *The*

Works of Sir Thomas Malory, ed. Eugene Vinaver (London: Oxford University Press, 1954), p. xvii.

[13] The phrase is the title of a volume on late English knighthood by Arthur B. Ferguson (Durham, N.C.: Duke University Press, 1960).

[14] *The Works of Sir Thomas Malory,* ed. Eugene Vinaver, 3 vols. paged consecutively (Oxford: Clarendon Press, 1947), p. 120. Subsequent quotations from the *Morte Darthur* are from this edition.

[15] Lewis, "The English Prose Morte," p. 9.

[16] Vida D. Scudder, *Le Morte Darthur of Sir Thomas Malory* (New York: E. P. Dutton, 1921), p. 201.

[17] Caxton, "Preface."

[18] Charles Moorman, *The Book of Kyng Arthur* (Lexington: University of Kentucky Press, 1965).

[19] The reader is directed to the exhaustive researches of R. S. Loomis and the other Celticists for a demonstration of how this conversion of myth into romance is accomplished. See particularly Loomis's *Celtic Myth and Arthurian Romance* and the appropriate chapters of *Arthurian Literature in the Middle Ages.*

[20] See Moorman, *The Book of Kyng Arthur,* pp. 28–48.

[21] Thomas L. Wright, "The Tale of King Arthur," in *Malory's Originality,* ed. R. M. Lumiansky (Baltimore, Md.: Johns Hopkins Press, 1964), p. 15.

Index

Achaean: defined, 10; first war
council of, 5; confederacy of,
10, 11; mentioned, 2, 8, 9, 36
Achilles: mythological origin of,
12–13, 14–15, 21; quarrel with
Agamemnon, 2–4, 15, 20, 22;
wrath of, 2, 3–4, 5–6, 22; as
hero, 3–4, 5–6, 15–16, 21–22,
25; heroic values of, 13, 15,
21–22, 168; and Hector, 5, 15,
16–17, 21; and gods, 25;
compared to other heroes, 13–
14; in *Odyssey*, 44, 45, 54;
mentioned, 10, 26, 27, 29, 59,
84, 88, 127, 133, 137, 143, 163
Aeolus, 37, 38, 40
Aeschylus, 26, 27
Agamemnon: as commander, 3,
6, 10–11, 12, 15, 20–21, 22,
25; quarrel with Achilles, 2–4,
15, 20, 22; as historical
character, 11, 12; heroic values
of, 20–21, 22, 168; in *Odyssey*,
44, 45, 54, 55; mentioned,
26, 27, 60, 82, 84, 115, 168
Aias: in *Iliad*, 15, 17; in *Odyssey*,
44, 45, 46; compared with
Achilles, 16
Aidos, 4, 12
Andreas, 78
Aneirin, 149
Anglo-Saxon Chronicle, 61
Annales Cambriae, 150
Annales Royales, 88
Anticleia, 42, 43, 44
Aphrodite, 18, 25, 59
Apollo, 2, 11, 12, 14

Ares, 14, 24, 25
Ari, The Learned, 140
Arthur, origin of, 148–49; as
historical character, 150–51,
167; birth of, 151; death of,
150, 151, 152; heroic values of,
167, 168; and Christianity,
150; mentioned, 156, 163, 169
Arthurian Chronicle Tradition,
151, 152, 153, 160
Arthurian legends: origins of,
154–55; beginnings of, 151;
growth of, 150; modern, 169
Arthurian Romance Tradition:
origin of, 154; beginnings of,
155; growth of, 158; characteristics of, 153–54; mentioned,
160, 165
Ate (Blind Folly), 24, 26
Atreus, 3, 11
Athene: in *Iliad*, 3, 4, 18, 22, 24;
in *Odyssey*, 47, 49–50, 53, 54,
55, 56; mentioned, 133
Atla Kvidha, 115

Babenbergs, 117
Badon Hill, Battle of, 149, 150,
151
Bear's Son's Tale, 51
Bede, 62, 63
Bédier, Joseph, 90, 91, 92, 93
Beowulf: and the Germanic
heroic ideal, 66, 67, 70, 79;
heroic values of, 66, 67, 70, 72,
75, 168; as ruler, 71–73; origin
of, 83–84; death of, 81, 84; as
pagan king, 79, 86; as

185

Christian, 68, 81, 86; and Grendel, 67; and Breca, 66, 67; and Grendel's dam, 66, 67; and Frisians, 67, 70; compared with Hrothgar, 68, 73, 75; and Onela, 72; and Hygelac, 72; and fate, 80; compared with Odysseus, 84; compared with Achilles, 84; mentioned, 94, 127, 133, 137, 143

Beowulf: origins of, 62, 65; structure of, 65, 66–68, 78; themes, 66, 85, 168–69; as tragedy, 75, 77; as Christian poem, 69, 76–78, 81, 85; as pagan poem, 78–81; Christian vs. pagan values in, 82, 83, 85; pessimism in, 77, 80–82, 85; heroic values in, 66, 67, 72, 75, 81–82, 84, 85–86, 167, 168; oral tradition of, 85; compared to *Iliad* and *Odyssey*, 81, 83, 86; compared to *Judith* and *Andreas*, 76; compared to *Nibelungenlied*, 86; mentioned, 80, 115, 116, 119, 122

Blackburn, F. A., 76
Bloomfield, Morton W., 76
Bowra, C. M., 5, 15, 24, 94
Briseis, 2, 3, 4, 6, 12
Brodeur, A. G., 68, 76, 79
Bruce, J. D., 155, 159
Brunanburh, Battle of, 61
Brunhild: origin of, 112, 114; character of, 114; death of, 111; and Kriemhild, 121, 124; mentioned, 111, 113, 120, 131, 136
Burgundians: court of, 112, 121; vs. Saxons, 113, 124; destruction of, 115, 116, 120

Calchas, 3, 4
Calypso, 33, 47, 48
Camlann, Battle of, 150, 152
Cantilenae, 89, 98
Capetian: period, 98, 101; kings, 97, 106
Carmen de Prodicione Guenonis, 89

Carmina, 90
Carolingian Period, 89, 96, 98
Caxton, William, first editor of *Morte Darthur*, 162
Celtic myth, 148–49, 154, 160, 167
Chadwick, H. M., 76
Chambers, E. K., 74, 151
Chansons de Geste, 89, 90, 91, 92, 93, 94, 95
Charlemagne: in battle, 87–88, 94, 104–105; sword of, 93; and Saracens, 106; death of, 95; and Baligant, 106; court of, 104; heroic values of, 168; mentioned, 90, 169
Charybdis, 40, 50
Chaucer, Geoffrey, 133
Chivalry: and courtly love, 153, 160; in Malory, 152, 162–64, 170; heroic values and, 165; in Icelandic sagas, 141; in *Nibelungenlied*, 118, 119, 128, 131; failure of, 129–30, 131, 164–65
Chrétien de Troyes: *Erec and Enide*, 121, 155; *Yvain*, 121, 155; *Cliques*, 155; mentioned, 154, 155
Christianity: and chivalric code, 170; in *Morte Darthur*, 169, 170–71; in Arthurian legends, 150; in *Song of Roland*, 99, 105, 106–108; in *Beowulf*, 74, 75–76, 77, 78, 79, 80, 81, 82, 83, 85, 86; in middle ages, 80; in England, 62, 80, 83; in Norse sagas, 134; and heroic poetry, 132
Chryseis, 2, 3, 12, 17
Circe, 32, 33, 38, 39, 40, 41, 43, 46, 48
Clarke, Howard W., 31, 46, 53
Collingwood, R. G., 149, 150
Comitatus code: in *Iliad*, 22; in Arthurian legends, 167; in *Beowulf*, 60–61, 63, 64, 67, 70–71, 75, 79, 83, 85; mentioned, 65, 68, 96, 168
Constantine, 153

Conte del Graal, 158, 159

Conteurs, 152, 155

Courtly love: characteristics of, 157; in Arthurian legends, 157, 158, 160, 164, 166; in *Song of Roland,* 97

Cuchulain, 13, 14

Cyclops, 36, 37, 40, 48

De Mirabilibus Britanniae, 150

De Vries, Jan, 91

Dietrich of Berne, 115, 119, 122, 126, 129

Diomedes, 15, 16, 17, 22, 23

Diu Nôt, 116

Dream of the Rood, The, 77

Elder Edda, 115

Eleanor of Aquitaine, 152

Elpenor, 32, 33, 41, 44, 46

Egils Saga, 140, 142, 144

Einhard, 87, 88, 90

Eris (Strife), 24

Eurylochus, 39–40, 42

Fate. *See* Moerae; Wyrd

Fates of the Apostles, The, 77

Feudalism: in *Song of Roland,* 95–97; and nationalism, 102–104, 105; in Germany, 117

Frazer, Sir James, 73

Frederick Barbarossa, 117

Ganelon: betrayal, 95, 99; trial and defense, 103, 105; mentioned, 102, 107

Gawain: origin of, 154; revenge of, 170; and chivalric code, 170; heroic values of, 168; mentioned, 152, 161, 163, 165, 166

Gentilesse, 118

Geoffrey of Monmouth, 148, 151, 152, 153

Geste Francor, 90

Ghibellines, 117, 118

Gildas, 149

Gilgamesh, 13, 14

Gisla Saga, 135

Godar, 137–38

Gododdin, 149

Gormont and Isembart, 92, 93

Graves, Robert, 19, 26, 51

Grendel, 74, 78, 79

Grettis Saga, 135, 142

Guelphs, 117, 118

Guillaume de Toulouse, 91, 93

Guinevere: marriage of, 151; and Lancelot, 157, 164, 165, 170; mentioned, 166

Gunnar, 86, 141

Gunnlaug Saga, 134, 135

Gunther: origin of, 115; character of, 122, 129–30; mentioned, 111, 112, 114, 120, 121, 123–24, 128, 129, 136

Hades, 14, 39, 41–44

Hagen: character of, 122, 128, 129; death of, 126; mentioned, 111, 112, 113, 114, 118, 120, 121, 123, 136

Hague Fragment, 92

Hallberg, Peter, 139

Hamilton, Marie, 76

Harold Fairhair, 137, 140, 144

Hastings, Battle of, 108

Hector: duel with Achilles, 5; character of, 16–17; compared with Achilles, 16; and fates, 25; mentioned, 6, 22, 27, 88

Helen, 11, 12, 25, 26, 27

Henry II, king of England, 152

Henry V, king of England, 162

Hen-Thorir Saga, 135

Hercules, 14, 46

Hermes, 38, 47, 54

Heroic Age: values of, 22, 60; in Greece, 9

Heroic literature: characteristics of, 28, 58, 59–60, 171; tragedy in, 168; Anglo-Saxon heroic tradition, 153; Germanic heroic tradition, 85; and Icelandic sagas, 147, 148; and *Nibelungenlied,* 120, 127

—Code: in *Song of Roland,* 108; in Icelandic sagas, 141; in *Nibelungenlied,* 112, 113; in *Odyssey,* 54–55; in *Iliad,* 22; in *Beo-*

wulf, 66, 67; failure of, 132, 146, 171
—Values: and heroic literature, 171–72; and history vs. myth, 169, 171; in Christian literature, 169; conflict of, 22–23, 166–67, 170, 171; in *Iliad*, 4–5, 20–22, 168, 171; in *Odyssey*, 52, 53, 54–55, 56, 84, 168, 171; in *Beowulf*, 66, 67, 72, 75, 81–82, 85, 167, 168; in *Song of Roland*, 106, 107–108, 167, 168, 171; in *Morte Darthur*, 166–68, 170; in Icelandic sagas, 143–44, 145; in *Nibelungenlied*, 116, 171
Hesiod, 9, 19, 20, 26
Historia Britonum, 149
Hohenstaufens, 117
Holmes, Urban, 92
Holy Grail: origin of, 167; legend of, 158–59, 159–60; compared with courtly love, 160; quest for, 160, 164, 167–68, 169, 170; knights of, 158; tradition of, 165
Holy Roman Empire, 96
Homer: 18–20, 40, 57–58, 122, 133, 147
—*Iliad:* as epic poem, 4–5; as narrative story, 2; as moral poem, 25–26, 59, 82; structure of, 2, 5–6; and history, 7–10, 11, 17–18; sources of, 7, 11; and mythology, 20–21, 28; and fate, 25–27; thematic range of, 5–6, 20, 26, 28, 59; heroic values in, 4–5, 20–21, 28, 168, 171; and theology, 23–26, 27, 28; mentioned, 57, 58, 59, 81, 83, 85, 94, 148
—*Odyssey:* structure of, 30, 33, 34–35, 47–48, 52; proem in, 30–32; invocation of, 30; as retrospective narrative, 34–35; as personal narrative, 35, 40; as moral poem, 59; themes, 30–32, 45, 59; heroic values in, 52, 53, 54–55, 56, 84, 168, 171; compared to *Iliad,* 36, 37, 38, 51, 53, 55–56; mentioned, 57, 58, 59, 81, 83, 85, 120
Homeric Age, 19–20
Homeric Question, 5
Hrafnkels Saga, 135
Hrothgar: as historical character, 83; as king, 72, 79; speech on humility, 67, 78, 79; and Beowulf, 67, 74–75; compared with Agamemnon, 84; mentioned, 61, 65, 66, 67, 70, 74
Hubris, 6, 21, 24, 26, 49, 114, 127, 128, 137, 168
Hygelac: origin of, 115; and Frisians, 70, 83; death of, 65, 67, 168; mentioned, 61, 62, 75
Hyperion: 33, 42; oxen of, 32, 42

Ionia, 10, 19, 23, 24, 57
Ismarus, 31, 32, 36, 48
Ithaca, 30, 35–36

Jones, George Fenwick, 102, 107
Jongleurs, 89, 91
Judith, 76, 77

Kaske, R. E., 76
Kennedy, Charles, 79
Ker, W. P., 66
Klaeber, Fr., 76, 79
Knights of the Round Table: origin of, 167; adventures of, 155–56; compared with Achilles and Roland, 163; heroic values of, 165, 166, 170
Kriemhild: character of, 120, 123, 124, 125–26, 127; revenge of, 115, 116, 120, 124–25, 126; grief of, 121–22; as epic hero, 127; and Brunhild, 111, 121, 124; and Hagen, 122, 124, 127, 129; compared with Lady MacBeth, 126; compared with Achilles, Beowulf, Roland, 127; mentioned, 111, 112, 114, 118, 119, 121, 123, 126, 131, 136
Kudoimos (Turmoil), 24

La Queste del Saint Graal, 170
Laertes, 36, 43, 54–55

Laestrygonians, 32, 37, 48, 50
Lancelot: origin of, 154; and
    Guinevere, 157, 164, 165, 170;
    exile, 166; and Christianity,
    169; and chivalric code, 170;
    and courtly love, 166; heroic
    values of, 165, 166, 168, 170;
    mentioned, 155, 157, 158, 163
Laxdoela Saga, 134, 135
Layamon, 153
Lewis, C. S., 161, 163
Lot, Ferdinand, 92
Lotus Eaters, 37, 48
Loomis, R. S., 160

Maldon, Battle of, 61
Malory, Sir Thomas: and chival-
    ric code, 162–64; character of,
    161–62; compared with Homer,
    161; and Christianity, 169, 170;
    purpose in writing *Morte Dar-
    thur*, 164; mentioned, 148, 161
—*Morte Darthur*: sources of, 170–
    71; heroic values in, 166, 168,
    170; contrast of values in, 165,
    166–67; and oral tradition, 161;
    and Christianity, 169, 170–71;
    as tragedy, 164, 165; men-
    tioned, 148, 162
McNamee, M. B., 75
Menelaus, 5, 11, 15, 19, 26, 53
Moerae, 26–27, 82
Murray, Margaret, 73, 74, 80
Mycenaean empire, 8–10, 19, 57,
    60

Nationalism, 106, 167, 171
Nennius, 149, 150
Nestor: compared with Agamem-
    non, 17, 23; mentioned, 3, 4, 6,
    10, 11, 16, 57
Nibelungenlied: sources of, 116;
    dates of, 118, 120; structure of,
    119–20, 127; foreshadowing in,
    121–23, 134–35; heroic values
    in, 116, 171; characterization
    in, 122–23; themes, 119, 120,
    122, 127; oral tradition of, 116;
    chivalry in, 119, 128–30, 131;
    mood and tempo in, 119, 121–

22, 131, 132; and religion, 133;
    contrast of courtly and barbaric
    values in, 118; fate in, 136;
    compared to *Beowulf*, 116, 132;
    compared to *Song of Roland*,
    107, 116; compared to *Odyssey*,
    120, 132; mentioned, 86, 112,
    118, 122
Njal: death of, 142; compared
    with Flosi, 143; sons of, 142; as
    pagan hero, 86; prescience of,
    135
Njal Saga, 86, 135, 140, 141, 144–
    45
Nordal, Sigurd, 139
Norns, 134, 136
Norse saga: dates of, 139; origin
    of, 139; sources of, 140; heroic
    code in, 141, 142, 146; heroic
    values in, 143, 144, 145; Norse
    hero, 123, 137, 141, 146; fate
    in, 135, 136; foreshadowing in,
    134–35; pessimism in, 134, 141;
    Christianity in, 134; chivalry in,
    141, 142; structure of, 144–45;
    themes, 145; compared to *Beo-
    wulf* and *Nibelungenlied*, 134;
    mentioned, 107, 110, 119
Northumbria: government of, 63;
    consolidation of, 63, 83
Nota Emilianense, 89, 90, 98

Octa, son of Hengist, 149
Odysseus: origin of, 51; wander-
    ings of, 30, 31, 32–33, 35, 48; in
    Hades, 41–47, 59; as king, 31,
    33, 48–49, 50, 51, 53; destruc-
    tion of suitors, 49–50; death of,
    43; as hero, 36, 37, 38–40, 46–
    48, 49, 52, 55, 60; and heroic
    values, 84; mentioned, 133. *See
    also* Scylla; Cyclops; Aeolus; El-
    penor; Polyphemus; Circe;
    Laestrygonians; Charybdis; Lo-
    tus Eaters
—in *Iliad*: compared with Aga-
    memnon, 17–18, 23; compared
    with Achilles, 36, 39, 49; men-
    tioned, 10, 15, 16
Offa, King, 62, 64

Oliver: character of, 98, 100; attitude of poet toward, 102–103; in battle, 99–100; death of, 91; compared with Roland, 98–99, 101–103; mentioned, 95, 168

Oral tradition: in *Iliad,* 9; in *Odyssey,* 57; in *Beowulf,* 85; in Arthurian legends, 161; in *Song of Roland,* 90, 91, 94, 95; in Icelandic sagas, 139, 140; in *Nibelungenlied,* 116; mentioned, 171

Otto I, 117, 131

Paganism: Germanic, 73–74, 80; Nordic, 134; in Britain, 80; in *Beowulf,* 78–81

Paris, 5, 19, 26, 27, 82

Paris, Gaston, 89

Patroclus, 5, 6, 15, 21, 24, 29, 113

Pauphilet, Albert, 92

Penelope, 42, 44

Perceval, The Story of the Grail, 155

Phaeacia, 30–31, 48

Philip of Flanders, 158

Philip of Swabia, 118

Phobos (Fear), 24

Polyphemus, 32, 33, 36, 37, 38, 42, 50, 52

Poseidon, 24, 33, 36, 37, 40, 43, 47, 50, 59

Priam, 15, 16, 22, 25, 26, 27, 127, 168

Pseudo-Turpin, 89, 90

Pylos, 8, 53

Raglan, Lord, 111

Rajna, Pio, 89

Robert de Boron, 159

Robertson, D. W., 76

Roland: character of, 94, 98, 99, 100–101; in battle, 99–100; as feudal hero, 101–102, 106, 107–108; and heroic code, 108; heroic values of, 167, 168, 171; death of, 89, 91; compared with Oliver, 98–99, 101, 103, 106; compared with Hotspur, 99; compared with Achilles, 88,

106; mentioned, 93, 94, 98, 102, 113, 123, 127, 137, 143, 163

Roman de Brut, 152

Roncevaux, Battle of, 88, 90, 93, 98, 105, 106

Round Table: origin of, 152, 153; fall of, 160, 165, 169, 170; mentioned, 152, 156, 168

Rudiger: character of, 130–31; death of, 131; as hero, 86, 130, 133; mentioned, 122, 126, 129, 131, 136

Saxo Grammaticus, 116

Saxons, 149, 150, 151, 154

Scylla, 32, 33, 38, 40, 48, 50

Siegfried: origin of, 111, 112, 114; legend of, 111, 118; character of, 112–13, 120–21; and heroic code, 112, 113; and Saxons, 113, 124; death of, 111, 114–15, 120–21; and Kriemhild, 113, 120, 124, 136; and Brunhild, 120, 124; and Gunther, 112, 120; compared with Achilles, 13, 14, 112, 117; mentioned, 86, 118, 121, 128, 131

Sisyphus, 46

Solar mythology, 14, 21, 47, 154

Song of Roland, The: date of, 88, 97; history of, 87; origins of, 89–91, 95, 106; battle in, 98, 104–106; other versions of, 88–89; structure of, 99, 104–106; themes, 98, 106; feudalism vs. nationalism in, 102–104, 105; traditionalists vs. individualists, 89–91; as Christian poem, 106–108; refrain of, 95; poet of, 91, 94; oral tradition of, 90, 91, 94, 95; heroic values in, 106, 107–108, 167, 168, 171; compared to Homeric epics, 94, 108; compared to *Beowulf,* 94; compared to *Iliad,* 94; compared to Norse sagas, 107; compared to *Nibelungenlied,* 107; mentioned, 93–94, 116, 122

Song of William, 92, 93

Spenser, Sir Edmund: *The Faerie Queene*, 108, 171
Stanford, W. B., 45, 51, 52
Sturlung Age, 138–39, 145
Sturluson, Snorri: *Prose Edda*, 134; mentioned, 73, 134, 138
Suite du Merlin, 170

Taillefer, 89, 108
Telemachus, 30, 33, 45, 53–54, 55
Themis (Order), 25–26
Thetis, 13, 18, 24, 25
Thidrandi Thattir, 135
Thidreks Saga, 110, 112, 115, 116
Tolkien, J. R. R., 66, 79
Trojan War, 7, 8, 9, 11–12
Trojans, 5, 133
Troy, 5, 9, 26, 35–36, 37, 48, 57, 59, 82

Turpin, Archbishop, 91, 101, 107
Turville-Petre, G., 139

Virgil: *Aenied*, 151
Vita Caroli, 90

Wace, 152, 153
Waltharius, 115
Wanderer, The, 61
Weston, Jessie, 160
Whitelock, Dorothy, 76, 77, 80
William of England, 155
William of Malmesbury, 89
William of Orange, Cycle, 91, 92
Williams, Charles, 169
Wyrd, 79, 82

Ynglinga Saga, 73

Zeus, 14, 18, 24, 25, 26, 36–37, 55